Mending Fences
Healing Hearts

The Top 10 Keys to a Better Relationship with Your Adult Children

Dr. Chuck Lynch

Mike —
Thank you dear friend
for all you have done
to make this project
possible
Chuck Lynch
10/25/11

ISBN: 1463507429
ISBN-13: 9781463507428
LCCN: 2011908698
CreateSpace, North Charleston, South Carolina

Dedicated *to*

DeeDee Lynch Neir

Michelle Lynch Peterson

Mom and Dad's adult children mentors

Turtle Acknowledgements

How did the turtle get on top of the fence post? It's obvious he did not get there by himself. That's how I feel. This effective tool for parents of adult children was not completed by the author alone. How can I begin to thank the scores of people who read and reread the manuscript? There will be stars in Linda Hight's crown for the countless hours of word processing the many revisions. Not enough can be said for my dear friend and colleague, Dr. Ron Neer, who managed the ton of details with the publisher. To top it off, my number one cheerleader and encourager, my wife Linda, patiently edited, proofread, and challenged me to think through each issue. My name may be on the book as the author, but I'm really just the turtle on the fence post.

—Chuck Lynch

INTRODUCTION

Mending Fences Healing Hearts

The Top 10 Keys to a Better Relationship with Your Adult Children

Here's some good news. It's not too late! You *can* improve your relationship with your adult children! Yes, your stomach churns over their bad choices. You didn't raise them to be that way! Your heart aches as they engage in self-destructive behavior or they've just added one more toxic relationship to their friend list. You may be in shock as you watch them pile up credit card debt while making little or no effort to find a job. You're frustrated observing them sit around spending countless hours texting, social networking, and playing mind numbing video games.

When you encourage them to move out on their own, you are met with guilt ridden accusations that you're "kicking them out." They refuse to respect your house rules and feel like martyrs if you ask them to help with the chores. Or you discover to your dismay that they're living with someone and having your grandbabies with no plans to get married.

Efforts to try to talk only erupt into shouting matches and now they don't call or come around much. The knot in the pit of your stomach doesn't go away and discouragement feels like your only companion. You're overwhelmed with feelings of hopeless resignation. "What's the use? Nothing seems to work. Now what?"

Mending Fences Healing Hearts starts right where you are. The first step is to restore your perspective. You are done parenting. Now, you must view your kids as adults…like God does, even if they don't act like adults. Failure to grow up does not excuse a person from adulthood.

From a renewed perspective, take the next step. It's a hard one. Choose to talk to them adult-to-adult rather than parent-to-child. That one change has mended many relational fences. Talking down to them doesn't motivate them to grow up. Learn a simple way to give advice even when they don't ask for it and open their closed minds. You will be able to respond appropriately to them when they don't choose to follow your advice.

One thing that tears you up is their failure to fulfill your expectations and dreams. It is possible to adjust your expectations to current reality and gain some welcome relief. Remember, you did the best you could with the information and maturity you had when you raised them, but, like us, you made mistakes. You will discover how to give and receive forgiveness from the heart and not be controlled by guilt and regret. The slate can be wiped clean. You will understand how important it is to distinguish between forgiveness and trust in rebuilding relationships. Now's the time to get off the emotional roller coaster and regain some emotional stability yourself.

You do love your kids, but they may not feel it. Learn how love them from their perspective in a healthy way. Plus, feel how good it is to establish healthy boundaries and then watch what happens through the power of personal responsibility. Financially, you've worked hard for what you have today. Grasp a simple method of dispensing your resources wisely and you will stop feeling like a walking ATM for your adult children.

Grandchildren are the joy of your heart, however, the way they are parented or not parented can be a source of grief. Learn how to be a wiser grandparent, regardless of what others are doing. Yes, every relationship has conflict. That's not bad, but how you deal with it can be. Follow four keys to deal with conflict and enjoy personal peace, even if no one else changes.

Mending Fences Healing Hearts is written plainly from both a professional and a biblical perspective, filled with real life case studies. It's easily understood and full of common sense. The questions at the end of each chapter are provided for small group discussion.

Discover for yourself that it's not too late to mend fences, heal hearts, and *enjoy* your adult children.

—*Chuck Lynch*

Table of Contents

CHAPTER 1

Get a Fresh Perspective

It was a late November afternoon when Pastor Robert and his wife Bev called my office. "Chuck, sorry to bother you," Robert began slowly. "Bev and I are at our wit's end. Our oldest daughter went away to Bible College and the next thing we knew she was not in college but was with some guy way out in California. She received a generous inheritance from her grandmother for college and now she has blown the whole thing with this guy. She won't listen to us. She says it's her life. She wasn't raised like this. We don't know what to do. Should I resign my church? Could we meet with you when we come to Kansas City?" He stopped suddenly with a flash of insight, "I think Bev and I just need to get our perspective back. We don't know what to do."

This is a familiar refrain echoed by parents of adult children in a relationship crisis with their kids. Grown children sometimes make bad choices, engage in self-destructive behaviors, develop unhealthy relationships, abandon any and all responsibility, pile up credit card debt, and don't want to find a job. They won't move out on their own, they won't listen to advice, or they're living with someone and having babies with no plans to get married. Parents cry out, "This is not the way it was supposed to be!"

The most frequently asked question by moms and dads in turmoil over their grown children is, "What can we do?" Yes, there are other questions, "Where did we go wrong?" "Why are they acting like this?" "Why don't they listen to us?" These questions probably reveal a deeper fear: "Don't they care about us anymore?"

These are all legitimate questions that beg for some answers, but a bigger task must be accomplished first. Pastor Robert said it best, "We need to get our perspective back." The very first step toward the goal of building a better relationship with your grown children may be for you to step back and get a realistic perspective of yourself, your kids and life as it is now.

Realize You Did Your Best

You may have forgotten how hard it really was to parent your children when they were growing up. Few things in your life were as challenging. Authors, Campbell and Chapman, write, "The choice to be a parent was the choice to have your heart walk outside your body for the rest of your life."[1] When the Apostle Paul was speaking to the new Corinthian believers about marriage, he warned that they would face many troubles (I Cor. 7:28). Although he was not specific, you can guess that one of the hardships he was referring to might have been parenting.

But take a step back. Despite the pressures you faced when the kids were little, you probably did the best job of parenting you could with the information, maturity and wisdom you had *at the time.* And yes, you probably did make a few mistakes. What should you do about them now? In chapter

5, we'll go into a positive strategy for correcting them. But for now, just recall how little preparation for parenting you actually had. You may have had more training to learn how to drive a car than you did to rear a child, yet how much more eternally important is it to raise a child? But you are not alone. Few parents are fully able to be the kind of parents they desired to be and are often painfully aware of their lack of knowledge and experience. They just did the best they could to meet the needs of the kids God entrusted to them.

The fact is that no parent, however kind, loving, or considerate can fully meet all of his/her child's basic mental and emotional needs. Thus all children arrive in adulthood lacking something. However, as they allow Jesus Christ to fulfill them, they will stop using childish, immature ways to face life's pressures.[2] We have all made mistakes and all children have suffered in some way because of them, but as long as we keep God in the picture, acknowledging Him in all our ways, He will make our crooked paths straight (Prov. 3:5-6).

Accept the Fact They Are Adults Now

So now that you have accepted the first perspective of understanding that you did the best job you could of raising your children, with the knowledge and maturity you had at the time, it is important to acknowledge that, like it or not, they are adults now.

Robert and Bev's college-age daughter had the age and appearance of an adult. But as I heard them describe her, it sounded like they were talking about a teenager. It was at this point I asked them to take a reality check, "Do you view your daughter as an adult, albeit a foolish one?" Glancing at the floor and slowly nodding their heads, they assured me that they knew she was an adult.

"Why the hesitation?" I asked.

"Well, we want God's best for her, but she is not making good decisions and we need to make sure she doesn't mess up her life."

"And you can do that?" I asked.

"We're her parents. She needs to listen to us and she's not acting like the way we raised her!"

Instead of answering them right away, I watched them. I could tell that they were listening to themselves and their minds and their emotions were colliding.

As a pastor, Robert knew it was God's plan for their daughter to experience the freedom, responsibility, consequences and rights that define adulthood. Yet he and Bev were reluctant to watch their daughter make different choices from those they believed were the right ones.

When one set of adults (parents) deny another set of adults (grown kids) their rights, responsibilities and consequences, conflict is bound to follow.[3] That's exactly what was happening. Robert and Bev had to learn the hard way the three words that define adulthood: *choice, responsibility* and *consequences.*

When parents are forced to confront this reality, they sometimes react by saying they love their kids and they can't stand to let them make these bad choices. But parents need to be reminded of a divine reality: God gives their children freedom of choice, responsibility for their choices and allows them to experience the consequences of those choices. He does this within the parameters and protection of His personal and perfect love for them (Gen. 2:17).

Only when you release your children to God's care are you less subject to the emotional roller coaster existence in which your moods are dependent on your kids' behavior. Instead of pushing them away from sinful choices, the pressure you project onto them because of your frustration or feelings of helplessness may actually drive them farther from God. Some parents have discovered that when they've released their children to be adults, they can relax and love them without being possessive (Joshua 24:15).

Robert and Bev's parental instincts rightfully wanted their daughter to avoid the pain that she was heading into at full speed. Parents can spare themselves a great deal of anguish if they accept the reality that when adult children have the right and responsibility to do whatever they decide, they also are entitled to experience whatever problems result. Acknowledging those rights gives your kids the freedom to make their own decisions, including bad ones. Failing to grant your adult children freedom to make independent decisions may be an indication of your lack of confidence in the way you prepared them for adulthood. You may bear some of the responsibility for that failure, but it is correctable. God gives you biblical tools to heal and improve relationships. Remember this important first perspective: *you did your best.*

Recognize Hindrances to Their Growth

It is God's plan for your grown children to become responsible adults and put away immature ways (I Cor. 13:11). If they have not grown up and are still emotionally immature and dependent, they may be going through "adult adolescence," physically grown up but behaving like teenagers.

It is estimated that at least 40 percent of current young adults (18-40 years of age) are excessively dependent.[4] Why is this the case?

Physically and Spiritually Lazy

Unfortunately, some young adults are physically and spiritually lazy. Who has taken over the T.V. remote and become the couch king? Some young adult "couch potatoes" are repeatedly met with the statement, "You are not trying hard enough to get a job." They may react like martyrs when requested to do simple tasks like mowing the yard, helping with house work, cleaning up their room or giving a hand in the kitchen. Unless they're clinically depressed, this behavior pattern is pure laziness which can be a form of denial. Change is difficult for all of us and it can be hard for adult adolescents to look inside themselves and admit their own lack of maturity. What do they do to avoid looking? They bombard their senses with T.V., movies, parties, computer games, Internet, music or any other stimuli that dull their senses. They may use excessive sleep, alcohol, or drugs to anesthetize any pain, shame, guilt, fear or boredom they feel.

Fearful of Responsibility, Failure and Rejection

Taking responsibility for choices and the ensuing consequences can be scary. To be accountable for those choices can be absolutely terrifying to an adult child. He wonders, "What will happen if I make a wrong choice?" Perhaps while growing up, he did not make enough decisions to learn that the world would not come to an end if he made a mistake. Or maybe there were plenty of opportunities but he failed to exert his faith and grow. Now he may be deeply fearful that he does not have the skills to deal with life's challenges, so he feels incapable of making decisions and living with the results.

Along with the fear of responsibility is the fear of failure. Hiding behind the fear of failure is another fear that comes from a lie deep within the heart that says, "If I fail at something, I will be rejected." Some parents may have delivered that message because of their conditional love and performance-based acceptance of their children. Regardless of how that lie became a managing principle of their lives, it is the responsibility of the adult child to identify and reject the lie and to replace it with truth (2 Cor. 10:4,5).

Fearful of Independence

The fear of independence leads immature adult children to avoid any effort to meet their own emotional or physical needs. They think they need someone else to take care of them. If they place this expectation on the parents, a love-hate relationship can develop: "I love you for who you are, but I hate you because I am dependent upon you." These grown children who choose not to leave home are called "nesting adults." They may have a deeply buried fear of being independent and alone, so they choose to stay in the "nest" where it is secure. They expect their parents to do only what God is responsible to do: be there all the time, know what they're feeling, and meet their needs (Heb. 13:5; Phil. 4:19).

Admit Your World has Changed

Another perspective that you may find hard to accept is that your world has changed, *drastically*. In general, people do not like change and loss. However, there are at least three major changes you have to acknowledge and accept and then change your perspective!

- Your world has changed.
- Your roles have changed.
- Your influence has changed.

The world you knew and tried to pass along to your children no longer exists. When you were a child, you lived in a social universe as different from your children's world as your own was from the world of Julius Caesar's.[5]

The Apostle Paul warned of at least 19 changes we can expect to take place in the end times (2 Tim. 3:1-5). Although many of these conditions have always been around, their scope has increased and intensified. God is allowing evil to take its natural course until His return. There will be degeneration, collapse and melt down in every sector of society, much more so than when you were a child.

This reality was hard for Robert and Bev to accept. Periodically they would shake their heads and bemoan how it used to be when they grew up, how their parents acted and what they could or could not do. But they failed to take into account just how much has changed since then.

For example, the financial picture is less predictable. Jobs and retirement are not secure anymore. Loyalty to an employer is a rarity because the employer may sell the company out from underneath them or they may face massive layoffs. As a nation there is more concern with money and the power it brings and the things it can buy than there has been in recent history.[6]

The only absolute is that there are no moral absolutes. There are few shared values. It is normal to have live-in relationships because marriage is too risky, fueled by the high divorce rate. We even hear the term "starter marriage" used to describe a first marriage. Extermination of unwanted people, referred to as abortion, is as acceptable today as the extermination camps were in Nazi Germany during World War II.

And who would have guessed that we, as a nation, would come to the place where we would debate the definition of marriage? The abominations of Sodom and Gomorrah are portrayed as normal acceptable behavior at every turn. Society reveres homosexuals and reviles the Boy Scouts of America.

Socially, the Judeo-Christian culture is on a high-speed collision course with secular forces and other world religions. Single-parent homes are about to outnumber dual-parent homes, reflecting the high divorce rate. Day-care has replaced parental care because of economic demands for two incomes. The church, rather than being a change factor for culture, has been permeated by the influence of worldly thinking (Rom. 12:2). This has resulted in tremendous psychological fallout of more anxiety and fear. The Food and Drug Administration has now approved antidepressants for kids that were previously prescribed only for adults. Coupled with record levels of depression is a fatal pessimism along with greatly elevated levels of anger. This anger plays out on the road, in sports, at school and at work.

Your children have been molded by influences that you did not have to face and they may be scared, depressed, anxious or even hopeless. Here it is important to remind yourself that God has given to each generation everything they need for life and godliness (2 Peter 1:3). Adjusting your perspective on these realities and conveying your understanding to your adult children can go a long way in building a mutually enjoyable relationship with them.

Realize Your Roles have Changed

One question parents inevitably ask themselves is, "When do we stop raising our kids?" Then follows other questions. "What is our role now that they are adults, at least physically?" "How have our roles changed?"

One of the hardest changes of perspective is the change of roles. Biologically speaking, you will always be your children's parents. That never changes. But now that they are adults, you have a responsibility to stop parenting them as if they were still a child. Shift your perspective from a parent to a mentor, guide and wise friend. Think of it this way: positionally, you are a parent, but functionally, you are a mentor. This means letting go of your image as "the parent" and your adult child as "a child." The reverse is also true. The young adult has the responsibility not to "play child" anymore.[7] Their rights and responsibilities should exactly mirror your own. This means they are allowed to be independent enough to be able to outgrow your views of authority (Matt. 12:48-50).

Your son is a man, possibly a husband and father. Your daughter is now a woman and perhaps a wife and mother. Both of them have rightfully shifted their loyalty from you to their spouse and their children. This reflects the leave-and-cleave principle in Genesis 2:24. Your son's role now is to sacrifice his life for his wife and she is to respond in submission and respect (Eph. 5:21-33). If you still want to parent your adult child, ask yourself two questions:

1. *Have You Accepted the Change?*

One of the reasons young people have a hard time separating from their parents or desire to return home to live is often the inability of the *parents* to adjust to the transition.[8] Why? You may want to stay in a role that makes you feel loved, comfortable and needed, even if that role is old, outdated and in need of desperate change. A changing role may seem scary because of a fear of the unknown or of being alone. You may rather put up with an unhappy relationship with your kids than make a major change in your perspective. God has promised that the joy and love that can come with the changes based on His Word are worth more than any cost the change might exact.

2. *Do You Still Need to Control?*

The second question to ask yourself focuses on the need for control. Power struggles and control issues lie at the heart of most family problems.[9] Attempts to control can reduce confidence, insert deep insecurity and generate anger between you and your grown child. Parents who do not respect the healthy limits of their grown children may not want to take responsibility for their own lives, so they take the easier path of dominating others. Chapter 6 explains how to take back control of your own life.

If you are reluctant to release control, is your personal security still wrapped up in your role as a parent? This dependency is not a family problem, it's a spiritual problem. If you are building your life around someone or something you are still trying to control, you have set yourself up for a lifetime of fear. Choose instead to build your life around your personal relationship with Jesus Christ and you will have will have a depth of security beyond human understanding (Gal. 2:20; Col. 3:1-4). Your shift in perspective is to believe with all your heart that your God (not your child) will abundantly supply all your needs (physically, emotionally and spiritually) in direct proportion to His glorious riches in Christ Jesus (Phil.4:19).

Your Influence has Changed from Protector to Mentor

What parent would not want to protect their child from harm? That's normal. Ultimately, you cannot protect your adult child from harm or the consequences of his own decisions. Even if you make their decisions for them, will that prevent them from making mistakes? This presupposes that only you, the parent, knows best. But, you are not all-knowing. You do not know what the adult child feels, thinks and needs. The Apostle Paul made this same point in I Cor. 2:11, "Just as you do not know the thoughts of God unless His Spirit reveals it, no one can fully fathom the thoughts of another person unless he himself tells it."

You do not know the destiny your grown kids will follow. Samson's parents had the same dilemma with their adult son. They knew that God had told them to raise him to be a godly

Nazarite (Judges 13:2-5). But Samson chose to disregard his parents' counsel to marry an Israelite. Instead he chose to marry a woman from the enemies of Israel, the Philistines, even though this was expressly forbidden by God (Ex. 34:16).

Samson told his dad, "Get her for me, for she pleases me well" (Jud. 14:3). The author of Judges adds this commentary, "But his father and mother did not know that it was from the Lord – that He was seeking an occasion to move against the Philistines - for at that time the Philistines had dominion over Israel" (Jud. 14:4). God was going to use Samson's rebellion for His own purpose and glory although that rebellion ultimately cost Samson his life (Jud. 16:28-31).

You still may want to protect because you lack faith in your adult child's ability to make decisions that you believe are good or correct. They will make a lot of mistakes just as you did when you were learning and maturing. Be their cheerleader rather than their critic. You can say, "What a learning experience!" In chapter 3 you will learn how to give advice and stand a better chance of having your advice heard.

A paraphrased principle of scripture for parents: "Unless the Lord guards and protects my children, I, as their parent, am attempting to protect them in vain" (Ps. 127:1). Worry is facing a present or future situation with God removed from the picture. Your need to control and protect will diminish as God is welcomed into your fears - and faith begins to dominate. Then, the peace of God which goes beyond your understanding will guard your heart (emotions) and your mind (thinking) through Christ Jesus (Phil. 4:7).

Create a New Climate

Your new perspective is clear. You cannot forcibly create a good relationship with your grown children, but you can help create a climate in which a great relationship can develop.[10] You are now able to distinguish between your ability to change your adult children and your ability to influence them. You now know the law of power: you only have the power to change yourself (and you know how hard that is); you cannot change another person. As a mentor you have the privilege of guiding them, but ultimate change is God's responsibility. Why? Because the motivation to change must come from within them, not at the persistent suggestion from well-meaning parents. God is the One who is at work *both* to will and to do of His good pleasing (Phil. 2:13), even if your sons or daughters are not believers or are not walking with the Lord.

It's time for you to consider praying Reinhold Niebuhr's 'Serenity Prayer',

> "God, give us grace to accept with serenity the things that cannot be changed, courage to change the things which should be changed, and the wisdom to distinguish the one from the other."

Change is hard for anyone. Now is the time to adjust your perspective to match God's perspective (Is. 55:8-9). The benefits of adjusting your perspective are enormous. Such an alteration could start you on a more enjoyable relationship with the people you dearly love. It could usher in some long-desired peace of heart. It could be just the ingredient that God would use to bring greater joy to you and to your grown children, as well as greater glory for Himself.

It wasn't easy for Robert and Bev to step back, re-evaluate and then change long-held beliefs. But to their credit, they did. Subsequent phone conversations only confirmed the reality of their hard work. As they changed their perspective, I shared with them ten important keys for establishing a healthy and enjoyable relationship with their daughter. The following chapters spell them out in detail. The first key was the hardest for Brandon and Sherry.

CHAPTER 1

Points to Ponder

1. Purpose to adjust your perspective to match reality.
2. Accept the fact you did your best with the information, maturity and wisdom you had at the time.
3. Remember you are dealing with a sin principle in both you and your kids.
4. Understand your primary role-model in parenting is how God relates to us as a Father.
5. Accept the fact your grown children are adults, for better or for worse.
6. Allow them to keep growing.
7. Give your grown children the same rights and responsibilities you enjoy as an adult.
8. Adjust to the reality that the world as you knew it has changed forever.
9. Shift your role from parent to mentor.
10. Release your grown children from the responsibility for your security.
11. Trust God for the ultimate protection of your grown children.
12. Choose to create a climate for good relationships.

CHAPTER 1

Get a Fresh Perspective

Small Group Questions

1. What perspective have you had to change as a parent of a grown child? What struggles did you go through to make these changes? How did you accomplish it? Who helped you? What resources did you use?

2. How did your parents respond to you when you reached young adulthood? What did they do that was helpful? What did they do that was not helpful? What do you wish they would have done differently?

3. How has your parenting differed from your parents? What were the factors that caused you to make the change?

4. Based on what you know now, what are some things you wish you knew when you were raising your kids?

5. Who were the most influential role models you had while raising your children? What did they model for you? How did it affect your parenting?

6. What are the hardest adjustments you have made in order to have a better relationship with your adult children? What process did you go through to accomplish that? How did your Christian faith enter into those adjustments?

7. How do you feel this changed world system has impacted your adult children? How have they dealt with it? How has it impacted your relationship with them?

8. What steps have you taken to deal with immaturity in your grown kids? What was the result of those steps? What do you wish you had done differently? What suggestions would you pass on to others?

9. How do you see your role now in respect to your adult children? How has this impacted your relationship with them? What did you have to go through to accept these new roles?

10. What are the hardest losses you have had to accept? What did God teach you about Himself and you through it?

CHAPTER 2

Communicate Adult-to-Adult

Brandon and Sherry have been our friends for years. But their visit to my office today was not a social one. The bottom had just fallen out of their relationship with their 33-year-old, single daughter Jennifer, who had just matter-of-factly announced to them that she was pregnant.

"We just don't get it," Brandon blurted out. "Jennifer has had everything. She was popular in high school and was the backbone of the church youth group. She had high morals and high standards for the guys she dated. She has a master's degree, a great job, and a great apartment. She's been lying to us about this guy she met at work. She said they were just friends. Now we've discovered he's not only fathered this kid, but other kids, too, and has never married any of the women. She expects us to just accept this? Now they're talking about just being friends. He's not interested in marriage. She just wants us to act like this mess is normal."

Sherry began talking through the flood of tears and streaming mascara, "All our dreams, not just ours but hers, too, are trashed. I've told her over and over again for months that this guy is a 'user' and a 'loser'. I've made it real clear what she should do. I used to call her or she called me every day, sometimes two or three times a day. Now there are just shouting matches. We keep trying to tell her what she needs to do to get her life back on track. She just tunes us out. We can't talk!"

Whether it's because of a crisis like Brandon's and Sherry's or just the day-to-day stuff of relating to adult children, I keep hearing the same thing repeated, "We just can't talk. We just get into arguments. We don't know how to communicate and the stress of a crisis doesn't help matters either." The result of strained relationships because of poor communication is distance, emotionally and physically.[11]

The first part of our time together with Brandon and Sherry was spent in helping to put the painful events into a healthy perspective, to invite God back into the picture and begin the healing of their hurts and disappointments. But there was a practical task that needed to be accomplished, too, and it wasn't going to be easy for them. I'm talking about the first key to establishing and maintaining healthy adult relationships with our children.

Shift to Adult-to-Adult Communication

The problem with Brandon's and Sherry's communication style with Jennifer was that it reflected a parent-to-child relationship. Unintentionally, they had failed to make the mental shift to that of adult-to-adult. This had to change.

According to Dr. Eric Berne, we communicate from one of three different reference points: we can talk adult-to-adult or we can talk parent-to-child. The third option is for the parent to talk to their child like the child is the parent and the parent is the child.[12]

In order to establish healthy communication with Jennifer, Brandon and Sherry needed to shift from viewing her as a child to regarding her as an adult, whether or not she acts, thinks or responds as an adult. This is the only way they can build a healthy relationship with her and encourage her to mature. They must resign the parent-child perspective once and for all. Parents must not wait until their children are acting, thinking and reasoning as adults before they speak to them on an adult level. It is your responsibility to cooperate with this God-designed maturing process, as all believers are instructed to do in (I Cor. 13:11).

As I conveyed this concept, the bewildered look on Brandon's and Sherry's faces said it all: "What does this adult-to-adult communication look like? How do we deal with all of Jennifer's stuff on an adult-to-adult level? How do you talk adult-to-adult with a 33-year-old who is going on 16?" Let's look at some communication styles that should be used, even if or when your child is not responding maturely.

Demonstrate Genuine Respect

Valerie Wiener, in her book *The Nesting Syndrome*, observed that every opportunity for problem solving between parents and grown children must start with mutual respect.[13] Maybe you think respect is a gift your adult child does not deserve, but that is the essence of grace: granting unearned favor to one who does not deserve it (see Rom. 11:6; Eph. 2:8,9).

You may have to fight off the impulse to degenerate into an angry little child yourself when your offspring acts like a child. Disrespect for them never develops their respect for you. There are few scenes that are more pathetic to watch than that of a shouting match between a parent and child. Your anger will never cause him to grow up and it will not bring the respect that you want from him. Respect that is demanded will evaporate quickly, but respect that is earned will endure for a lifetime. Wise parents will remain in control of their feelings in the face of foolishness (Prov. 26:4) and will refuse to return insult for insult (I Peter 3:9). Now, let's look at ways you can demonstrate genuine respect.

Respect Their Feelings and Opinions

Doctors Ross and Chapman believe the first and most powerful way to demonstrate respect for your adult children is to place genuine importance on their feelings and thoughts or at the very least to acknowledge them.[14] One practical way to do this is to show deference to their wishes. For example, if your married kids prefer that you call them before you pay them a visit, do it! Treating them with consideration will go a long way in conveying that you value and honor them. Brandon and Sherry's daughter expressed just such a need to me. Weeks after I met with Brandon and Sherry, I met with Jennifer. She openly acknowledged her wrong choices and was prepared to take full responsibility for the consequences of her behavior. She shared her hurt. "Mom and Dad never give me credit for anything I do. I have a master's degree and a successful career. But if I have an opinion different from theirs, I'm the kid, I'm wrong. They're the parents; they're right. Sure, I have made big time mistakes. But I'm never allowed to have an opinion or feeling that does not meet with their approval. I don't expect them to agree with me, but I would at least like for them to acknowledge my right to have an independent thought."

One of the benefits Brandon and Sherry would have gained by respecting Jennifer's feelings or perspective was that it would have informed them what she really had been thinking, even if it was just her perception of reality. To her, perception and reality are the same.

Let's say that your adult child expressed his belief that you showed favoritism to one of his siblings over him. You can win if you can respectfully respond, "I acknowledge how you feel" or "Thank you for telling me how you feel. Your opinions and feelings are very important to me." Warning! Do not add a "but" and try to defend yourself or correct their perception by saying, "I acknowledge what you are saying but I think you are wrong." The word "but" automatically erases the words that preceded it and it devalues them and their feelings. You will not gain an honest relationship if you attempt to defend your past parenting. Instead, mirror back what you heard. "Am I hearing you say that you felt we showed favoritism to your brother over you?" After he responds ask him if he would be open to sharing with you more about that and what else he experienced as a kid. Then, be quick to listen and slow to speak (James 1:19).

If you think there were circumstances that would be helpful for him to know or understand, you can say, "Sometime, now or later, I would be open to share our viewpoint about those events, whenever it works for you." If you disrespect your adult child by discrediting, belittling, or shaming his perspective, he will quickly determine it is not safe to share his feelings or outlook with you and he will be reluctant to trust you again. The result is distancing. You may defend yourself to preserve your pride, but it could be at the expense of the relationship you deeply desire. You must respect his honesty and perspective.[15]

One relational bridge many parents seem to be unable to cross is honestly attempting to understand our adult child's perspective. The biggest reason is that we're so bound by our own outlook on life and what we believe to be best for our children that we find it almost impossible to see the world through their eyes.[16] Henry Wadsworth Longfellow wrote, "If we could read the secret history of our enemies (or adult children), we should find in each man's life sorrow and suffering enough to disarm all hostility."[17]

What kind of "sorrow" or "suffering" might you hear from an adult child who has not moved out of the house yet?

> "Stop pressuring me to achieve all the time."
>
> "Praise me when I do something well."
>
> "Tell me you love me, even if I act like I don't want to hear it."
>
> "Express yourself honestly. I don't like it when people lie to me."
>
> "Stop yelling. That only makes me angrier and more defensive."

> "Respect me enough to let me come up with my own opinions. I have to learn how not to agree with you and still have your respect."
>
> "Keep talking" to me. I like to know that the lines of communication are open between us. However, realize that I will not always want to talk when you are ready to talk. Be patient with me."
>
> "Realize I have reached adulthood and will have my own ways of doing things."
>
> "Respect me for who I am and realize that I need to make my own mistakes."
>
> "Understand that my generation is different from yours. This doesn't make me wrong."[18]

It is *crucial* that you acknowledge your adult children's viewpoints and feelings in order for them to feel respected by you. In time they may even change some of their opinions, just as you have. Always keep the communication channels open by showing sincere interest in what they share.

Make Requests, Not Demands

The second way you can demonstrate genuine respect is to make requests of your adult children like you would other adults, instead of making demands of them. No adult enjoys being told what to do. Demands and commands do not reflect an adult-to-adult relationship. Sometimes employment roles and responsibilities may place you in a position where this is necessary, but all of us recoil at a demanding attitude. In his first letter, the Apostle Peter urged church leaders, who had a great deal of authority and responsibility, not to "lord it over the flock" but instead replace lording with exemplary servant leadership (I Pet. 5:3). Illustrate to them how you want them to act toward you. Don't demand of them what you're failing to illustrate yourself. The elders were to be servant-leaders. You have the same task as parents to avoid exasperating your children with demands, whether they are kids or adults (Col. 3:21).

Demands or commands do not reflect respect in an adult-to-adult relationship. Demands usually reflect an effort by one person to control another. They may comply on the outside, but on the inside resides deep resentment.[19] Adult children feel like servants and not family.

When your children were young, you would pointedly tell them what to do. As they grew older you practiced asking rather than telling them to do something, hoping they would respond obediently and cheerfully. When our daughters were young and asked for something we would respond, "What's the magic word?" A "please" answer demonstrated respect to us. Just as it is common courtesy for adults to punctuate their requests with that word, so we should make it a habit to use "please" and "thank you" with our grown children.

One of the key lines that Linda and I use with each other and with our grown daughters when making a request is, "Would it work for you… to bring the books back sometime this week?" There is a biblical basis behind this style of communicating a request. When the Apostle Paul urges believers to be devoted to one another in brotherly love, he spells it out, "Give preference to one another in honor" (Rom. 12:10). Asking, "Would it work for you?" is just one small way of honoring their preference.

You cannot develop a mutually enjoyable relationship with your adult children without communicating on an adult-to-adult level. This is first characterized by genuine respect whether or not they act respectfully toward you. You may have to separate in your mind their "position" as God's creation and their "personality." Their responsibility is to respect you for your position as their parent. Your task is to earn respect; that's your responsibility. Often respect is demanded because there has been a failure to earn it. It is also your responsibility to model respect according to the standard Jesus set, "Therefore whatever you want men to do to you, do also to them..." (Matt. 7:12).

Control Your Anger

The first shift you may have to make in communicating adult-to-adult is to demonstrate genuine respect. The second is to stay calm by controlling your anger. Jennifer described a recent blowup with her mom. "I was explaining to my mom that I wanted my baby's father to be in the delivery room with me. She went ballistic! She ranted and raved at me how I shouldn't have anything to do with this creep, let alone allow this user and abuser to be in on the delivery. I expected my mom to disagree with me, but I wanted her to respect my wishes. Yet, every time I fail to agree with her, she turns the cannons on me and goes into a rage and blasts away."

"And how did you feel about her response?" I asked.

She rolled her eyes, exhaled deeply, glanced at the floor then slowly lifted her resigned eyes to meet mine and softly said, "I'm used to it."

"Used to it?" I replied.

"Yeah, I can't stand conflict. I always cave in when she gets mad. She knows it, too. I hate her for it."

When Jennifer announced her delivery plans, Sherry was understandably shocked and deeply hurt. However, her display of anger did nothing to build a good relationship with her daughter. If she had practiced some self-control, she would have invited love instead of rejection from Jennifer. Solomon declared, "He who is slow to anger is better than the mighty, and he who rules his spirit than he who takes a city (Prov. 16:32). Paul reinforced this in his letter to the Galatians where he lists self-control as the ninth fruit of the Holy Spirit (Gal. 5:23).

Sherry's response was not just a response to a recent event in the family; it was her pattern of control. She had used anger in at least three ways with her daughter. If parents use these same three approaches with their adult children, they may get the same response Sherry got: rejection, not relationship.

1. Do Not Use Anger to Control

Anger is a normal emotion. But parents, like Sherry, can misuse it in order to control their children. What motivates them to do this? Fear is one trigger. In Sherry's case, there was her fear of abandonment. Her first husband had deserted her when Jennifer was a toddler and she turned to her daughter for comfort, companionship and security. To ensure that Jennifer would not leave her, especially now that she was an adult, Sherry used anger as a tool of control rather than discover the historical source of her fear and deal with it. Where should Sherry have been looking for her ultimate security? Col. 3:3 says that our lives are now secure because they are "hidden with Christ in God."

Besides sabotaging relationships, the wrong use of anger damages the person himself. A chemical is released into the bloodstream which raises the fear level and reduces the ability to listen, concentrate and understand. Scripture tells us that love "casts out fear" (I Jn. 4:18), but did you know that the opposite is also true? Fear casts out love. Sherry was trying to grasp love, but her outbursts succeeded only in driving it away.

We should seek peace in our relationships because it is one of the fruits of God's righteousness. The Apostle James pointed out, "...the wrath of man does not produce the righteousness of God" (James 1:20). Sherry's fits of temper did not foster peace or acceptance.

2. Do Not Use Anger to Change

The second unhealthy use of anger is to try to change someone. Sherry wanted Jennifer to change her mind and not permit her ex-boyfriend in the delivery room. Jennifer wanted her mom there, but it was a "no way" situation with mom. She didn't even want to be in the hospital if that "creep" was going to be there. This time her anger was not working. It took some hard counseling sessions before Sherry was willing to accept the fact it was Jennifer's decision and to acknowledge it was God's responsibility to change Jennifer, not hers. Parents who believe they can mold their adult children into an image of their making are behaving selfishly and unbiblically. The only image God desires us to reflect is His image as seen in Christ (Rom. 8:29). The Apostle Paul sets an example for he told the Galatians, "I labor in birth again until Christ is formed in you" (Gal. 4:19). If the image the parent wants his or her child to reflect is like Christ, acting un-Christ-like toward your adult children will not do it! Using anger to change someone is never God's tool of choice for parenting. Force just produces resentment.

It is God's responsibility to work in your adult children's lives "to work and do of His good pleasure" whether they're committed believers or are backslidden (Phil. 2:13). The first characteristic of adulthood is choice - not yours, but theirs. Why? Because they are responsible for their choices and the subsequent consequences, not you (2 Cor. 5:10).

3. Do Not Use Anger to Manipulate

The third wrong use of anger is to manipulate another person into meeting your own needs. To change and control are the key tools of manipulation. Other means of manipulation are guilt, shame, fear, silence and threats of rejection, but anger is the one adult children report experiencing the most. Anger never produces healthy relationships. It is your task to choose to talk calmly, adult-to-adult and to retire the selfish tool of anger as a means of changing, controlling or manipulating your adult children.

Should you become angry while in an intense conversation with your kids, be adult enough to request a time-out to cool down and clearly re-think what is taking place. Make a firm commitment to return to the topic when a calmer spirit is in control. Reduced anger can calm a dispute (Prov. 15:18) and serve as a format to work through conflicts.

Encourage Often

Another way to promote mature interactions is through frequent encouragement. Even though Jennifer made plenty of wrong decisions, including sexual intercourse outside of marriage, she still had a deep need for encouragement. Whether our children's behavior is wrong or foolish, they have a God-designed need for encouragement (Heb. 3:13). Make encouragement a daily habit, not a daily sermon on avoiding sin. They need encouragement by your positive words, actions, choices or attitudes to keep doing the next right thing.

Our adult children are facing a tidal wave of negative influences in the culture, at home, work, school, play, and, yes, even at church. They need all the encouragement they can get. Your relationship with them can be more pleasant and satisfying if you focus on their accomplishments instead of their misfires. Replace criticism and condemnation with congratulations, praise and support, and see what a difference it makes.

A word picture from the Apostle Paul helped me form the habit of giving encouragement to our daughters. "Let no unwholesome word proceed out of your mouth, but only such a word as is good for edification according to the need of the moment that it may give grace to those who hear" (Eph. 4:29). The key word "edification" means "to build up." From it we derive our word for a building: *edifice.* In the first century the primary means of construction was brick, block, and stone. A building was erected one brick at a time.

My words I picture like building blocks. When doing a seminar on communication, I illustrate it by selecting someone from the audience and arranging four brick-size cardboard blocks in a square. They are asked to pick up a "brick", one at a time, and toss it across the room to form a square exactly like the one I made. It has never happened! In the same way, you have a choice to toss your words carelessly or place your words carefully. The outcome, according to the Apostle Paul, is that the one who hears our encouraging words will receive grace (or favor).

Wherever I go, I visualize pulling a red wagon full of word bricks. I can choose to toss a brick destructively (see Gal. 5:15) or purposefully. When we visit our oldest daughter's home, I look for things that are commendable and praiseworthy so that I can add a positive building brick to her life. Linda and I have this same attitude toward her husband, Roger, and the four grandkids. We want our family to know how much we value them and how proud we are of them.

Adult-to-adult conversation is mutually beneficial when words are help for the need of the moment and are viewed as a gift (Prov. 15:23). What if the words you need to share are hard to receive and are not viewed as a gift? At times like this you understand the value of a healthy adult-to-adult conversation, demonstrating respect, staying calm and giving encouragement. This may be easier to do compared to the next characteristic of adult-to-adult communication.

Listen More, Talk Less

Have you noticed that sometimes we as parents just talk too much? Good communication strikes a balance between speaking and listening, and this is especially important during conflict.

As Jennifer unraveled her deep feelings of love and frustration toward her parents, one thing kept resurfacing. "When my dad said he wanted to talk to me, he really meant he wanted to lecture me. He didn't want to talk 'with' me; he wanted to talk 'at' me. His mind is as closed as a steel trap. Conversation is supposed to be a two-way street. He doesn't get it."

Talking Is Not Listening

It sometimes puzzles people when I mention the importance of listening by saying, "Talking is not listening." If I were to ask Brandon if he spends much of his time in conversation with Jennifer listening, he would say, "Yes." Why? Parents usually think talking is listening, but the number one complaint of adult children is that their folks are poor listeners. The most important aspects of listening are patience and silence. This is hard because effective listening is putting your current feelings aside to hear how someone else is feeling (or thinking) at that moment.[20]

James emphasizes an important key to healthy communication, "But let everyone be quick to hear, slow to speak..."

(James 1:19). No one is excluded when he says, "Let everyone" which includes kids *and* parents. Proverbs is less flattering when it comes to an impulsive talker, "Do you see a man who is hasty in his words? There is more hope for a fool than for him" (Prov. 29:20). Let's look at some helpful approaches to productive listening for a mutually-satisfying relationship between parents and adult children.

Preparing Your Defense Is Not Listening

Most communication conflicts between parents and children are characterized by defensiveness. In fact, the urge to defend is stronger than the need to listen and try to understand what is being said. So, while your child is pouring out his heart in gut-wrenching pain, are you preparing a defensive comeback? No wonder parents are accused of being uncaring or unwilling to change. Proverbs is more specific when it comes to our impulsive talking. "He who answers a matter before he hears it, it is folly and shame to him" (Prov. 18:13).

Mirror Back

When Jennifer tried talking to her dad, if he would have repeated back what he heard her say, he would have made huge gains in their communication. This technique has been referred to as "mirroring back" and helps both the listener and the speaker. It reassures them both that they are responding to the same information and that it was understood.

Even after 49 years of listening to and sharing with people one-on-one, I still regularly check with counselees to make sure I have grasped what they have said. I have been wrong too many times to not continue this practice. It is simple: merely paraphrase what you think you heard your adult child say about any given point. You might start off by saying "Am I hearing you say ...?" He just might light up with excitement because he feels understood. And if you think this is only for the benefit of your son or daughter, let me hasten to say that it is enormously important for both of you. Your adult child will also be more responsive because he feels heard, and you will have more of an opportunity to be included in the confidence of a grateful and possibly relieved adult child.

Stick to the Topic

Responsible listening involves a conscious effort to avoid issue hopping, that is, jumping from one issue to another that may or may not have anything to do with the current topic of discussion.

When Sherry attempted to explain why she could not be in the same room with the guy that "used" her daughter, Jennifer shot back, accusing her mom of not liking any boy she dated. Then she proceeded to remind her mom what a jerk her first husband, Jennifer's father was. Notice what happened here. The first topic was Mom's reluctance to be in the delivery room with the baby's father, then it shifted to the topic of boyfriend selection, then it shifted to her father. Some have referred to issue hopping as going to the history channel and replaying the past to avoid dealing with the issue in the present. What should you do when that happens? Verbally acknowledge the new event or topic and affirm you are willing to discuss it at a later time, then return to the present issue.

What if Jennifer attacks her mother by stating she has never been there for her? Shouldn't she set the record straight? Yes, but not now. That is an important topic, but the tactic of issue hopping is often employed to avoid the guilt, fear, shame, or responsibility for a current issue. At all cost, be an adult yourself and stick to the topic at hand.

Many families are pulling 40-foot-long trailers full of past unprocessed issues because they fail to bring closure to issues as they come up. They seem to overreact to a present situation, but in reality, most overreacting is not overreacting; they are dealing with accumulation of long-standing unresolved matters that have built up over the years. With your adult child, avoid issue hopping or reverting to the history channel by chronically reminding them of their past failures. Stick to the topic. What if they don't want to discuss the current issue? They can choose to do that. You are free to end the discussion by stating you are willing to revisit the issue again on an adult-to-adult basis at another time.

Don't Interrupt

If you think avoiding issue hopping is hard, try holding your tongue while another person is in the middle of a sentence. Cutting someone off in the middle of a sentence is the clearest signal you are not listening but are planning your response to clarify or to defend yourself. It is a reversal of God's communication key, "quick to listen, slow to speak" (James 1:19) and instead, reflects a "quick to speak and slow to listen" pattern. Remember, listening includes understanding.

Often in marriage counseling while one spouse is speaking the other spouse will interrupt. I silently raise my palm toward the interrupter signaling them to wait until the other person is finished. Then, I thank the listener for waiting and remind them that listening is an important conversation tool. At the end of the session, I ask, "Were you able to express what you wanted to convey?" Many times the answer is "yes," followed by the comment that this was the first time they have been able to communicate adult-to-adult and be heard. You can expect this is the same response by allowing your adult children to finish what they are saying without being cut off. Constructive communication involves both senders and receivers.[21]

Avoid Below-the-Belt Tactics

In the book *The Dance of Anger,* Dr. Harriet Learner lays down many ground rules to avoid an angry response between family members. These below-the-belt tactics include shifting blame, interrupting, diagnosing, labeling, analyzing, preaching, moralizing, ordering, warning, interrogating, ridiculing, lecturing, and other put-downs.[22] These do not reflect adult-to-adult communication as much as sand-lot arguing. Low-blow tactics reflect little listening and very poor talking. This form of communication results in a relationship going from bad to worse.

It may be hard to believe the response you *could* get by demonstrating respect, staying cool, encouraging often and listening more. Yet, you can do all of this and still remain shallow but cordial in adult-to-adult communication. If you want to plunge deeper you must dive first and hope they will follow. How?

Admit Frustrations, Disappointments and Mistakes

Doctors Campbell and Chapman suggest the first step in deepening your adult-to-adult conversations is to honestly admit your own frustrations and disappointments with life and acknowledge that you have made some poor decisions, too.[23] I recall sitting on our married daughter's hunter green couch with my wife, Linda, reflecting back on our child-rearing years. We talked about the perfectionistic ways that caused us to be overly critical of her and how they instilled in her a fear of failure and the feeling that she couldn't do anything right. As we were open, honest and, yes, vulnerable to her potentially negative reaction, something else happened instead. DeeDee was free to share the mistakes she felt she had already made with her children. Linda and I had to take the plunge first. It was not that we never talked about our parenting mistakes, but as Linda and I continued to be open, honest, and saddened about those events, a deeper heart-to-heart, adult-to-adult communication slowly increased. Part of that vulnerability means that we allow our grown children to ask questions and receive honest answers about our past parenting. This is a crucial part of the healing process of any past hurts.

Acknowledge Your Own Struggles

Admitting past frustrations and disappointments is a good start. Now be real about today. Admit to your children that you struggle – I mean the real struggles. You had to be strong when your young children were vulnerable and impressionable. You were their anchor of life.

But now that they are grown, you are developing an adult-to-adult relationship with them and that means that you are to be honest with them about your own struggles in life. In fact, this is a prerequisite before you effectively give any insights you believe will help your children in their search for meaning in their life.[24]

The Apostle Paul did this in his mentoring. He looked back on his 18-month ministry among the believers in Corinth and when he could have reinforced his authority and prominent position as an apostle, instead he opened up his heart and reflected back on what he was going through at that time. He simply and humbly admitted, "I was with you in weakness, in fear, and in much trembling" (I Cor. 2:3). The Corinthian believers probably would not have known about his internal struggles if he had not told them.

Be Open about Your Past History

Admitting your frustrations, disappointments, and struggles in life is a good start in developing a deeper adult relationship with your child. Now go a little bit deeper. Be open and honest about your own history which includes your parents and grandparents. By sharing your own history, it will greatly help your adult child to understand how your self-image, attitudes, and beliefs were formed.[25]

God has a sovereign purpose for history. It is "His story" of His dealings with us and us with Him. The Apostle Paul explains one of the reasons God recorded the history of the Jews with all their flaws, "Now these things happened to them as an example, and they were written for our instruction, upon whom the ends of the ages have come" (I Cor. 10:11). To paraphrase this passage: these things happened from time to time and were written down from time to time for a specific purpose. What was the purpose? Simple, it was to teach us and to drive home certain lessons.

God does not waste history – either yours or others. Whether your history is good, bad, or ugly, there is something in it that God can use to teach you and your children. Some aspects of your life may not even make sense to your kids because they have no context for them.

A few months before my father died, I discovered something that had been hidden and right-out lied about for years. My dad had told me he did not know who his birth parents were and that he only knew his adoptive parents. He said the records were sealed. But, while going through documents as his legal guardian, I discovered his adoption papers and there in black and white, were the names of both his birth parents and adoptive parents. Then came another surprise. My dad's adoptive parents also adopted and raised my dad's birth father.

When I was in middle school, my father abandoned my two brothers and me. Dad had been abandoned by his birth father who had also been abandoned. Three generations in our family were affected by abandonment, underscoring what God said that the sinful patterns of the fathers affect the children to the third and fourth generations (Ex. 20:5). That revelation did not change my history, it did something else. It gave me a deeper understanding of the pain my dad experienced as a kid. I know my dad was wounded. Now I know the wound and a lot of things make sense and I have a greater peace with our family history.

One of the characteristics of an unhealthy family is the presence of family secrets which play a large role in family dynamics. Dr. John Friel, in *Adult Children,* mentions three characteristics of an unhealthy, dysfunctional family; they don't talk, they don't feel, and they don't trust. Being appropriately open and honest about your past can give your adult children a context for your life and their life and result in a deeper bonding. They are adults now. They can handle it.

Be Transparent

Nothing opens the door of your adult children's heart more than your honesty and transparency. Valerie Wiener explains, "Intimacy grows on the freedom to disclose personal information, personal opinions, and personal vulnerabilities." She describes the pay-off from this openness, "When one person listens, it encourages the other to share these personal parts of life."[26] Adult children respect those who are honest and transparent, and they are open to those they respect.

The word "transparent" comes from a prefix "trans" (over, across, through) and the word "parent." A parent should be transparent - appropriately open, frank, and candid about his past and present. This will greatly encourage your children to hear you say you don't know it all and that you are still a learner yourself. This levels the playing field of life. You have a wealth of life experience that they don't have and it has taught you a basic truth of life: the more you know, the more you realize how little you really know. That is where your kids are. They are overwhelmed with life, feeling they have so much to learn because they know so little.

Being transparent with your kids today just may be the key to open the door for them to give you some feedback about your parenting in the past. Your children know things about you that no one else knows. You know truths about them that no one else can share with them. What an incredible opportunity to learn about yourselves and each other, especially once you break down the barriers between you.

Take the First Step

What kind of messages have you been sending to your adult children by the way you communicate with them? Have you been talking at them as if they were still in diapers? (i.e., "my baby girl"). Have you been addressing them as though they were adolescents with one foot in adulthood and the other in childhood (i.e.., "Son, if I've told you once, I've told you a thousand times."). If so, is it time to rearrange your perspective to match God's? He views them as adults with responsibilities and consequences and with the right to make their own choices, just like the rest of society.

Take the first step to communicate with your children on an adult-to-adult level, even when they behave immaturely. Choose to deal with them as God does. He does not alter His Word or His ways for immature adults. The way you communicate adult-to adult may just be the key to encourage them to grow up to adulthood.

CHAPTER 2

Points to Ponder

1. Shift your communication style from parent-to-child to adult-to-adult.
2. Demonstrate genuine respect for their feelings, thoughts, and opinions.
3. Make requests, don't issue demands.
4. Control yourself and your anger.
5. Avoid using your anger to control, to change, or to manipulate.
6. Encourage them often.
7. Listen more and talk less.
8. Prepare your response *after* you have listened well.
9. Stay focused on the subject at hand.
10. Allow a whole thought to be expressed without interruption.
11. Fight fair. No low-blows.
12. Admit your frustrations and disappointments with life and God.
13. Acknowledge your own struggles
14. Share your past.
15. Be transparent.

CHAPTER 2

Communicate Adult-to-Adult

Small Group Questions

1. Describe a conversation impasse you have experienced with one of your grown children. What led up to it? How did it affect you? What were the steps taken to overcome it?

2. How have you changed your perspective to be able to communicate with your adult children?

3. On what levels have you communicated in the past with your grown kids (parent-to-child, child-to-parent or adult-to-adult)? How did they respond? How did you feel when you communicated on that level?

4. When and how did you make the shift from parent-to-child to adult-to-adult? What struggles did you experience in making the transition? What was the biggest obstacle you had to overcome to accomplish this?

5. When is it most difficult to grant your adult children respect? What did you do to make it possible or easier? How did they respond?

6. What emotions of your grown children are the hardest to respond to appropriately?

7. How have you demonstrated respect for your adult children's opinions, especially if you did not agree with them? How did they respond? How did you feel afterwards?

8. What has helped you in controlling your anger? What did you tell yourself? How did you learn to do this?

9. When has anger been used to control, change or manipulate you? How did you respond to it?

10. In what practical ways have you encouraged your adult children? What have been their responses?

11. What have you learned from your grown children by making a special effort to listen?

12. How have you shared your personal struggles with your adult children? How do you think it benefited them? What has it done for your relationship?

13. What in your parent's or your past history has been hard to share? How did you do it? What was the response? What did you learn from doing it? What is the next right step you need to take?

CHAPTER 3

Advise When Asked

When Mike and Vickie came into my office, the first thing I noticed was his dejected countenance. After a few pleasantries, I asked how I could help. Vickie reached over to squeeze Nate's hand as he looked up at me, slowly shaking his head. With a quick glance at Vickie, he took a deep breath, closed his eyes, and started to shake his head again.

"Why does this still bother me? I mean, uh, well you know, we just built our first home. We like the way it turned out. We did the landscaping, not the builder. Vickie and I dug, planted, edged, and did more digging and more planting. It looked great to us. Then we invited my dad over to look at it. Of the three kids, I'm the only one to have ever done this."

"Well?" I asked.

Mike dropped his head, bit his lower lip, took a deep sigh, and continued, "We walked around the house. Then Dad started up.

"'This bush was a poor choice to set off your entry steps. You planted that tree too close to the house. In ten years you'll be trimming it back.'

"My dad criticized every bush, plant, and tree, even how I had mowed the yard." He sighed again. "Why should I care what he thinks?" Raising his head slowly, his eyes met mine. Pleading in a soft voice, he asked, "Why can't I just get over it? It's been this way all my life. He's impossible to please. I have teenagers, and he still feels he has to tell me what to do his way."

Sometime later I received a phone call from a teaching buddy. It happened three weeks before we were scheduled to leave for Nigeria. "Hey, Chuck," he began, "I've got to back out of the trip. My daughter is expecting her fourth child. She and her husband are fighting like cats and dogs. They're always broke, hardly can afford diapers, and just bought a plasma TV with surround sound and no payments or interest for a year. I've tried a gazillion times to tell them how to get their marriage back on track and dig themselves out of the financial pit. You'd think they would listen to dear old Dad. My daughter just told me to bug off. I just feel I need to stay close, in case the lid blows off of this."

What parent has not wanted to give his kids advice, especially in a crisis? After all, you have learned at least a few things in life that you would like to pass on to your children, either to benefit them now or to prevent them from making the same painful mistakes you did. Besides, there's the adage that says, "A smart man learns from his mistakes. A wise man learns from the mistakes of others."

God does intend for our grown children to profit from our hard-earned wisdom. King Solomon said, "My son, hear the instruction of your father, and do not forsake the law of your mother; they will be a graceful ornament on your head, and chains about your neck" (Prov. 1:8,9). Then he added, "For length of days and long life and peace they will add to you" (Prov. 3:2). If only it were as simple as quoting this proverb to our kids!

My frustrated buddy asked me just before he hung up, "By the way, how do you get your grown kids to listen to you? Carrie and I feel so helpless!" Many people have asked me this a dozen different ways, but the underlying question is still the same, "What is the best approach to use when you want to give your children advice?" The answer is simple, advise when asked.

The next question I hear is "But what if they don't ask?" There are five things I share with frustrated moms and dads whose adult children obviously could use some direction, yet have tuned out their parents:

- Ask their permission first.
- Consider your approach.
- Allow them to take your advice or leave it.
- Give them room to learn in other ways.
- Keep the door open in case their way fails.

Ask Permission First

Before you share your pearls of wisdom with your children, make it a practice of asking permission first. There are good reasons for doing this.

It Opens the Door

Unwanted or unsolicited advice can shut the door of the mind, especially if there was not a previous pattern of mutual respect and trust. That's why parental lectures are so ineffective. The choice is up to you. Do you want to be heard and acknowledged or do you just want to get something off your chest? If you just want to feel better, it usually means that someone else is going to feel bitter.

It was obvious that Nate's dad only wanted to give his opinion without acknowledging any of his son's efforts or meeting his desire for an encouraging word from him. Words of admiration from a dad are like gold nuggets to a son.

How can you open your children's minds? One suggestion would be to first affirm or praise something positive (I Cor. 11:2). Don't dilute or erase the benefit of your praise by adding "but," and then proceeding to tell them what you think they ought to do. Let praise stand on its own. Then try saying something along this line: "May I offer a suggestion?" "Would you be open to a suggestion?" "May we share our perspective on this situation?" Even as a counselor, I do this with my clients. Then I wait for their answer before I go on.

It Allows for Immaturity

Sometimes people are just not ready to hear advice from others. My buddy's daughter and husband were not mature enough to practice delayed gratification. They saw what they wanted, bought it, played with it, and postponed payment for it. The consequences of their poor choices did not register, and they didn't want anyone to point them out. Her angry response to her dad was a defense mechanism for avoiding remorse, guilt, shame, or fear. If he had withheld a response until receiving a go-ahead from his daughter, my friend could have avoided the angry outburst and stopped the probable weakening of their relationship.

Jesus chose to withhold important information from His own disciples simply because they were not ready to receive it. "I still have many things to say to you, but you cannot bear them now" (John 16:12). Dr. Edwin Blum, commenting on this verse, observed:

> The disciples were not able to receive any more spiritual truth at that time. Their hearts were hardened; their concern was for their own preeminence in an earthly kingdom, so they saw no need for Jesus' death. Sorrow over His departure and dismay over the prophecy of a traitor among them, along with the prediction of their own desertion, rendered them insensitive to more spiritual truth.[27]

The Apostle Paul had to modify his counsel to the Corinthians because of their immaturity: "And I, brethren, could not speak to you as to spiritual people but as to selfish, as to babes in Christ. I fed you with elementary teaching and not with in depth teaching; for until now you were not able to receive it, and even now you are still not able; for you are still selfish" (I Cor. 3:1-3). Just as those people were influenced greatly by worldly thinking and behavior, so our grown children may be.

It Demonstrates Respect

Demonstrating respect is vital, so much so that I have made multiple references to it throughout this book. When you do not pressure your children to listen to your advice, but rather invite them to accept it from you, or even wait for them to ask you for it, you show them respect.

Just as we have locks on the doors of our homes to prevent intruders from entering, so we have boundaries in our lives that regulate how close we allow others to get. In the interest of building a better relationship with our children, we need to be sensitive to their limits; otherwise, we will be met with defensiveness.

If your grown children respond with "I'd rather not hear what you have to say about this," you can reply, "I'll respect your wishes." Doing so to their potential loss is very painful for you, but it is necessary for cultivating the kind of relationship both you and God desire. As you maintain this position, you will keep communication lines open. Then, if they change their minds about hearing your counsel, they will feel free to come back.

By asking permission first, you are conveying the understanding that they have control of the information gate of their minds and that they deserve this respect as adults. They are responsible both for what they choose to hear and what they refuse to hear. Ultimately, we are all responsible for our choices, as we are reminded in Romans 4:12, "So then each of us shall give account of himself to God."

It Creates Curiosity

Something else occurs when we have respectfully asked if they would be open to a suggestion. They become curious. Curiosity increases receptivity. A word of caution is in order here: questions that masquerade as a subtle form of interrogation are a guaranteed turn-off, such as, "May I ask just how you were able to pay for that?" Don't even think about going down that road.

If your grown children generally ask for your advice, consider yourself fortunate, and realize that you did many things right for you to have earned that privilege. At the same time, keep in mind that you may need to discern between their desiring direction and their avoiding responsibility to think for themselves. You can do this by inquiring what they think they should do or what they think their options are before you share yours. They just may need reassurance and not advice.

Consider Your Approach

After learning the value of gaining permission before we give our children advice, we need to look at *how* we request their permission and deliver our advice. Even before we speak a word, we are delivering a visual message. After all, more than half of our communication is conveyed through body language, and our children are "reading" us within the first three to seven seconds. Rolling eyes, furrowed brows, pointing fingers, and hands on the hips can all be expressions of exasperation, disapproval, accusation, or rejection. Adult children have told me that they don't like to be around their parents because of the negative looks they get.

Watch Your Body Language and Tone of Voice

Authorities in communication agree that our tone of voice and body language make up 93% of communication and the content is only 7%. I don't know what my friend's facial expression was when he talked to his daughter; but if the tone of voice I heard from him on the phone was the same he used with her, it's no wonder she turned a deaf ear to him. Adult children cringe when they hear parental undertones of anger, sarcasm, mocking, belittling, superiority, or disgust.

In contrast, an open face conveys a thousand unspoken messages. Something as simple as a smile can sometimes break through otherwise impenetrable barriers. Take your cue from God, who instructed the priests to pronounce this blessing upon His chosen people (Num. 6:24-26):

> The Lord bless you and keep you;
> The Lord make His face shine upon you,
> and be gracious to you;
> The Lord lift up His countenance upon you,
> And give you peace.

The phrase "lift up His countenance upon you" means "look upon you with favor." Even if you do not approve of the way your children are acting, grant them favor. This is what God does for you. Let your face beam, conveying that they are valuable to you. They certainly are valuable to God (see Luke 12:7).

One other thing about facial communication: eye contact is essential. Grown children grieve when parents either will not look them in the eye or look through them as though they weren't even there. King David, in Psalm 32:8, wrote, "I will instruct you and teach you in the way you should go; I will guide you with My eye." There is a difference of opinion about whether it is God or David doing the instructing. Either way, we can see the crucial role that eye contact plays.

We have emphasized the importance of body language (how we look) and tone of voice (how we sound) as we communicate with our children. Next, we'll look briefly at content (what we say).

Use Inviting Words

When asking permission to share your thoughts, phrase your words to sound like an invitation. Earlier, I suggested some approaches, and here are a few more.

> "May I offer (make) a suggestion?"
>
> "Would you be open to a suggestion?"
>
> "May I ask you a question regarding . . .?"
>
> "Would it be appropriate for me to offer (make) a suggestion?"
>
> "Are you open to discussing this?"
>
> "Did you want me to comment on this?"
>
> "May I suggest something for you to think about?"
>
> "May I share my perspective on this?"

Let your words reveal an attitude of respect and humility, while your face radiates genuine love and honor for them.

Clarify Fact from Opinion

When giving advice, learn to distinguish between fact and opinion. Your personal experiences and observations should not be equated with truth. Delivering your opinion as absolute truth reflects arrogance and a possible need to control. The root of control is not faith but fear. Being opinionated and fearful will only alienate your children.

Maintain a heart of humility. In sharing your opinions, you might say such things as these: "This is what I've experienced." "I had a similar situation to deal with one time, and this is how I handled it." "Now this may not be the only way to look at it, but one of the things I have observed is. . ."

Provide Scriptural Support

When you want to share a moral or scriptural viewpoint, be sure you have references to back it up. Just as we are to have a ready defense for unbelievers who want to know what we base our hope on (I Pet. 3:15), so we should be prepared to offer our children solid biblical evidence for our assertions. Truth stands up to scrutiny. The Christians in Berea were commended by Paul and Silas because the Bereans checked out in the scriptures everything Paul and Silas taught (see Acts 17:11). By all means, avoid any pretense of preaching or lecturing. Follow Jesus' example. He was conversational with Nicodemus (John 3) and with the Samaritan woman at the well (John 4).

Avoid expressing your opinion as though it were God's. One mother actually told her adult daughter, "I don't feel that God wants you to homeschool your children." She was entitled to express her preference, but using God to support her position was a major turn-off to her daughter. Avoid selecting an isolated verse and taking scriptures out of context in order to support your opinion. This is a selfish misuse of the Bible and has been referred to as spiritual abuse.

Make Suggestions Rather than Proclamations

It is best to relate to your adult children in the same manner you relate to your peers. In such a context the following words are inappropriate: *need to, should, ought to,* and *must.* Nate's father broke the first rule about giving advice to his son by not even asking his permission to do so. Then, instead of offering suggestions, he made critical pronouncements:

"You should have put more thought into where you located those trees."

"You need to replace those wood chips with rock in the flower beds."

"You ought to have known those plants won't do well in the shade."

"You must rethink your sprinkler system plans. They just don't make sense."

In the interest of keeping the door open with your children, use wisdom in your delivery. For example, say you are riding in your son's car and hear some transmission noise. Do you announce, "You need to get that transmission looked at before you get stuck on the road"? Or do you engage in a friendly dialogue such as this one?

You: "Sounds like you may have some transmission problems."
Son: "Yeah, it just started last week."
You: "Have you had a chance to get it looked at?"
Son: "No."
You: "Open to a suggestion?"
Son: "Yeah."

You: "I'm off tomorrow if you decide to get it looked at. I would be open to following you to the dealership, and if you need a car, you can use one of ours."

I think you would have to agree that this approach is more likely to be well received.

Differentiate Between Wrong and Different

When our daughters were born, the standard procedure was that dads and others remained in the waiting room. But at the birth of our four grandchildren, not only was our son-in-law in on the delivery, but we were, too. Is either of these practices wrong? No, they are just different from each other.

It's true that cultural values of the world have permeated the church so pervasively that often you cannot tell the difference between the two. However, some things merely reflect a change in taste or style. Many evangelical churches have adopted a more casual Sunday dress, contemporary music that targets a younger generation and a Saturday night service. It's not a matter of right and wrong. Before you jump to conclusions about the choices your children are making, ask yourself, "Is this a moral issue or a preference issue?"

The Apostle Paul addressed the "different" versus "wrong" thinking in the church at Rome. Some believers held that no day had any special religious significance, while others believed that certain days, like Sunday, were special. It didn't matter to Paul which position a believer held because it was not a moral issue. So he urged that "each be fully convinced in his own mind" (see Rom. 14:5).

A good rule of thumb is that where two opinions clash in matters that are not prohibited by Scripture, we need to show mutual respect. Making personal taste and preference a matter of right and wrong is a surefire way to alienate your children. Do respect their wishes, especially when you are in their home. By the same token, they are to respect your wishes when visiting your home. That mutual respect for each other's differences and preferences will greatly enhance your relationship.

Allow Them to Take Your Advice or Leave It

The third tenet to giving advice effectively is to let your adult children choose whether to follow your advice or not. This is hard to do. After all, you have a wealth of experience and information you could impart, saving them heartache, stress, and money.

Adulthood, as we have noted, is defined by at least three characteristics: choice, responsibility, and consequences. Your children are responsible for choosing what to do with your feedback, and they will enjoy the benefits or suffer from the consequences of their decisions. After you give your input, take your hands off. That's your responsibility. They can take your advice or leave it. If they know they have that freedom, they may feel more inclined to ask you the next time. Instead of worrying about your approval based on their decision, they are now free to evaluate and decide. Doctors Campbell and Chapman asked one adult child how she formed a close relationship with her mother. Her reply, "I think it's because Mom allowed me to grow up. She doesn't treat me like a child. She doesn't tell me what to do. Because of that, I respect her ideals. In fact, I often ask her advice. I don't think I would do that if she tried to control me."[28]

Our fellowship with God is based on our choice to obey or not to obey. Joshua spoke to the nation of Israel adult-to-adult and emphasized their right and responsibility to choose to follow God or not: ". . . choose for yourselves this day whom you will serve . . . . But as for me and my house, we will serve the Lord" (Josh. 24:15).

Respect is Not the Issue

Do you think that if your children fail to take your advice, they are disrespecting you? It could well be that they are functioning as adults and evaluating the advice they receive. Keep *who you are in Christ* separate from *what you do for Him* because you have been crucified with Christ and it is no longer you who live, but Christ lives in you; and the life which you now live in the flesh you live by faith in the Son of God, who loved you and gave Himself for you" (Gal. 2:20).

Emotionally Disconnect from Your Suggestions

It is hard to disconnect emotionally from the advice you give your kids. You don't want them to hurt. You feel their pain. That's OK. You are their parents. Look at the role you and God play in evangelism. You can the plant the seed and even water it, but can you make it grow? The hard part is to stand back and wait for God to cause it to grow (see I Cor. 3:6-7).

You want to see the results of years of emotional, financial and spiritual investment in your children's lives. The waiting is so hard. It boils down to what you believe about God. Do you trust Him and what He is doing in their lives or do you feel you have to step in and help God out?

When your adult children disconnect emotionally from your advice, it's your opportunity to continue to love them and trust God to accomplish His ultimate will, regardless of how they respond to you. They might openly reject your input, but that does not mean they don't want to hear it. Avoid this stubborn reasoning: "If they're not going to take my advice, I'm not going to give it to them." You don't know if or when your kids will choose to respond favorably to your advice. God gave His Word even when He knew it would be rejected. This was illustrated over and over again in the life of Pharaoh (Exod. 7-14) and Israel (Ezek. 2:1-8).

Realize, too, that those closest to you may have the greatest difficulty taking your advice. In fact, because you are family, there is a built-in, potential rejection factor. Jesus experienced this in His family. He said, "A prophet is not without honor except in his own country and in his own house" (Matt. 13:57).

Give Them Room to Learn in Other Ways

As much as you want your kids to learn from your mistakes, God has designed another method of teaching them; it's called "reproofs of instruction" (Prov. 6:23). King Solomon underscored the importance of parental instruction (Prov.1:8), which provides guidance, protection, and counsel. But when godly advice is not heeded, God brings reproofs or discipline to instruct and to correct. Discipline is for directional change. It comes from God's heart of love (Heb.12:6) and produces "the peaceable fruit of righteousness by those who are trained by it" (Heb. 12:11).

Let Go and Let Them Learn

Letting your adult child go is not abandonment. It is releasing him to be who God designed him to be: a responsible adult. You may not know what is best for your son or daughter. God may have a plan that you do not know about. Though you might like to step in and stop your child from making bad choices, such intervention may be an attempt to protect you from feeling his pain. Doctors Campbell and Chapman explain the irony of this thinking:

> Parents cannot bear the thought of a child - even an adult child - having any pain or problems out in the real world. Ironically, this is most prevalent in parents who have had to survive great hardship and have emerged as competent people. Instead of realizing that their hardships are what made them strong and competent, they desire that their children have problem-free lives with no character-building trials. They forgot that it takes preparation and training to be able to function and prosper in a world that is far from being user-friendly. Part of this training is to experience difficulty. There is no other way for children to learn to deal with the normal stress of life.[29]

Change Your Perspective on Their Trials

It is important to adopt a positive attitude about a seemingly negative situation. The son of our friends got arrested for drugs while in high school. When they told me about it, my first words were, "What a learning experience!" That did not exactly go over well initially. But the more we were able to factor God into the picture, the more potential benefits we could see. The judge held up his court hearing for a year. While he was waiting, the son stayed clean from drugs.

The Apostle James went a step further and urged us to welcome trials as friends because we know they will expand our faith and strengthen our emotional endurance (James 1:2-4). I personally believe trials are going to be a learning experience whether our adult children's trials are self-inflicted or not. Affliction can teach us God's statues (Ps. 119:71) or motivate us to obey His Word (Ps. 119:67). Either way, benefits abound.

Avoid Short-Circuiting the Learning Process

When our sons and daughters are in trouble, our every impulse as parents is to step in and fix the problem. However, this short-circuits their learning process. A hallmark of their maturity is the ability to work through their own problems and consider appropriate counsel without their parents trying to rescue them.

I am reminded of an experience with our youngest daughter when she faced rejection in high school. Some of her classmates were not believers, and she had maintained a solid Christian witness before them. Thinking it was my job as a parent and a counselor to fix the situation, I prepared to charge in with my bag of tools. But Michelle looked at me through tear-filled eyes and firmly said, "Dad, you can't fix it!" I swallowed hard, took the reproof, and admitted,

"You're right." I just hugged her and let the tears flow, both hers and mine.

During her college years, she knew we were there for her. In each challenge she faced, her words echoed in my ears: "Dad, you can't fix it." When I would ask her what she needed, her answer was often simply, "Your love and support." Honestly, it is harder to give love, acceptance, and encouragement than it is to jump in and attempt to solve the problem. But when you give your grown children the freedom to take whatever course of action they feel is appropriate, this confirms to them that you believe they are adults.

Distinguish Between Influence and Change

As a parent of two grown daughters, I have often wanted to step in and do something to change a situation. Though it's not easy, I realize that my ability to effect a change is limited to influence. You and I are in an incredible place of influence with our children. Our task is to accept the fact that we cannot change anyone, children and spouses included.

One way to tell whether we understand the difference between influence and change is our frustration level when our children don't listen to us and do as we say. If we get frustrated at those times, we probably are failing to recognize their right to make their own choices. We are deceiving ourselves if we believe that if they just follow our advice, everything will turn out all right.

Sons and daughters have repeatedly told me that they feel smothered by their parents' manipulative ways. Such efforts to control are motivated by fear on one hand and fantasy on the other. Fear reflects some unmet emotional or spiritual need in the parents, and fantasy reflects the delusion that parents can change their adult children into what they think is best. Take a step back for a moment and affirm that you are in a godly position of influence, not change. Change is God's job (see Phil. 2:13). Our job is to sow and water in people's lives, but He causes them to grow (see I Cor. 3:6-7). When you feel frustrated, see that as a positive reminder that you may be trying to make them grow instead of sowing and watering through your influence. By choosing to use influence instead of control, you are leaving the decision to your children about whether or not to change. Ultimately, you are trusting God for the results.

A few months after my teaching buddy and I had talked, I asked how he and his wife were doing with their daughter who had told him to back off. He was a different person. He sounded less stressed. I detected a change of heart. He said, "My daughter is right. It's her life, her kids, her husband, her choice. Carrie and I are just going to love them, encourage them, be there for them, pray like crazy, and let them be adults." Advising only when asked will reinforce that same reality for you.

CHAPTER 3

Points to Ponder

1. Realize that you have a wealth of wisdom to pass on.
2. Ask permission to share it first.
3. Focus on opening the door of their minds before you speak.
4. Discern whether they are in a place to hear your advice just yet.
5. Respect their refusal to listen.
6. Create curiosity by asking questions.
7. Evaluate your body language, tone of voice, and what you say.
8. Maintain an open face of acceptance backed by your love.
9. Look at them when you talk.
10. Clarify that your advice is your perspective.
11. Give them the freedom to take or leave your advice.
12. Support your viewpoint with facts.
13. Avoid preaching and lecturing.
14. Distinguish between "wrong" and "different."
15. Emotionally disconnect from your suggestions.
16. Give them room to learn in other ways.
17. View their problems as learning experiences for them.
18. Do not short-circuit their learning experiences.
19. Distinguish between influence and change.

CHAPTER 3

Advise When Asked

Small Group Questions

1. How did your parents attempt to advise you? How did you feel when they did it?

2. When have you wanted to say something to your children but sensed they were not ready or open to it? Were you able to share it later?

3. What have you found opens your adult children to receive your advice? How did they respond?

4. What adjusted your body language or tone of voice over the years? What has been the response to these changes?

5. How have you adjusted your thinking on "wrong" versus "different"? How did it happen? What was the response?

6. How did you come to the point of sharing your advice and then letting them take it or leave it? In what areas did you do this?

7. How have you disconnected emotionally from your suggestions? What did you tell yourself to be able to do this?

8. What lessons have you seen your kids learn apart from you? What was it like for you to watch it happen? What support did you have?

9. How have you shifted your thinking from trying to change your children to one of influence? What difference has it made in your relationship with them?

10. In what ways have you seen God work in your adult children's lives apart from your influence?

CHAPTER 4

Clarify Mutual Expectations

Linda and I were speaking at a marriage conference in a church pastored by a long-time college friend of mine. His oldest daughter had just been married the year before. Our oldest daughter was about to get married. Ralph looked over the breakfast table at me one morning to offer some practical advice on how to relate to our daughter and son-in-law after they were married. "Chuck, whatever you do, don't go over to their new apartment until they invite you. Let them get settled. Let DeeDee express her nesting instincts. When the nest is ready, she will invite you over."

After the wedding, we waited and waited. She and Roger had been to visit us many times, but there was no invitation to their home. Months later in a hurt tone of voice, DeeDee inquired, "Why haven't you come over to our apartment?" Linda and I exchanged shocked glances.

"Uh...we were waiting for you to invite us. We were told that is what newlyweds wanted." The disappointment in her eyes met the shocked look in our eyes. We profusely apologized. Was the hurt we inflicted intentional? No! But intentional or unintentional hurts feel the same. Something was very obvious; we had failed to clarify before the wedding what our mutual expectations would be after the wedding.

Unexpected Pain

Unfulfilled expectations are one of the top contributors to poor relationships with adult children, not just your expectations of them but their expectations of you. We never expected to cause the pain we inflicted on our daughter. Yes, it was a misunderstanding, but it was a misunderstanding of unexpressed expectations. She and Roger expected us to spontaneously just drop in for a visit. This would have shown them how happy we were with the choice they made of each other. It would have given us an opportunity to compliment them on their decorating. DeeDee excels in interior decorating. But our failure to understand their expectations of us, and projecting our expectations on them, resulted in mutual, unexpected hurt.

What is an Expectation?

Originally, the word "expect" merely meant to wait for something ("*ex*", out, plus "*spectare*", to look). It just meant to look for something as likely to occur or appear. The word grew to mean not just a passive waiting *for* something but an active anticipation *of* something. It expanded to mean there was a great confidence that a particular event would happen. Then it grew from anticipation of a possible event to a looking forward to something that was due or "owed." It has almost evolved into a rule that one person makes for another person.

Many arguments between adult children and their parents often use three key phrases, "you need to," "you should," or "you must." What started out as an anticipated possibility of a pleasurable event turned into a rule or law that must not be violated. It is no longer an option; it's a necessity. It is not to be a possibility or even a probability, it must be an actuality. For some, expectations are not just deep down hopes; they have come to mean "my expectations are also my due."

Why are expectations one of the top contributors to poor relationships with adult children? Either the parents or the kids have failed to give each other what the other feels is their due. Valerie Wiener would say expectations are "Rules about another person's life choices."[30] It is very close to giving orders. We have to distinguish in our minds whether our expectations are "wishes" or "rules."

I believe DeeDee was acting on the older meaning of the word expectations; to wait, look forward to something with pleasure and anticipation. We failed her. The wait turned into a feeling of rejection and disappointment. All of this because we failed to do one of the top ten things to build better relationships with grown children, clarify mutual expectations before the marriage Failure to honestly discuss expectations on an adult-to-adult level sets the stage for conflict, hurt feelings, withdrawal, arguments and revenge.

If you don't work out the parameters of your relationship together, there is a high probability that inaccurate assumptions will be made. Frequently, one person makes decisions based on what he *thinks* the other person wants or expects but judges the other person incorrectly. Part of the reason most relationships originally get into trouble is because people don't communicate clearly with each other."[31]

That is exactly what happened between DeeDee and us. We assumed that our perspective was hers, too, "Stay away until they're ready." She and Roger assumed we would drop by fairly soon to see them in their newlywed home.

Clarify Mutual Expectations

Everyone wants to win. No one wants to lose. One of the best ways to win with your kids and they with you is to clarify your mutual expectations. We finally did this with our daughter.

One evening DeeDee, Roger, Linda and I sat in their living room to have a family chat. Linda and I wanted to avoid more hurt by understanding their expectations of us. We all wanted to anticipate with pleasure our time together. That evening was really an eye-opener for Linda and me. They were open and honest with us. We all needed to make adjustments in our thinking to get on the same page in many areas.

Here are some topics to consider with your grown children, whether single or married.

Plan Ahead for Holidays and Vacations

Marriage and family counselors observe that one of the most volatile times of the year is the holiday season, especially between Thanksgiving and Christmas in the United States. Unresolved family conflicts that are ignored during the year seem to surface at that time. Expectations clash as to how those events should be celebrated and with whom.

When happy memories are associated with those holidays, the thought of them not continuing as they did in the past is hard to accept. It's a loss. It's a change, but we still think we can make it a family "rule" that we will be together! Ask your adult children how they visualize the holiday season so that you can discuss mutually acceptable plans. Because DeeDee's in-laws like to celebrate holidays with their son and grandchildren, too, we figure out a time to get together with our own family, whether or not it is on the actual holiday. It is important to clarify in advance the details about when and where to celebrate. Failure to do so guarantees a collision of expectations, resulting in unnecessary hurts.

If dinners are involved, it is important to clarify who brings what, who is going to serve and who is going to clean up. Large messes that are left to be cleaned up by the "willing" hosts may cause them to smile on the outside but seethe on the inside.

Do you expect your kids to come over every Sunday for dinner? Do they expect to be able to do so? One of our close friends complained that they could not do anything on Sunday afternoons because their son and his wife expected to come to their home every week for dinner, unless their kids had other plans. During an honest adult-to-adult conversation they discovered that each one thought the other one expected it. The tension eased immediately when they both shared their thoughts and discovered they were misreading each other.

Your single kids may want to go to a friend's home, take a trip or bring a boyfriend or girlfriend home for the holiday. If they are living together, clarify before the visit what each other's expectations are for the sleeping arrangements. In the case of a lesbian daughter or homosexual son who wants to bring their partner home for a visit, talk adult-to-adult and clarify what you expect or don't expect during that visit. Again, the rule for all holidays is simple. Ask on an adult-to-adult level what your kids expect from you and you from them. Be prepared to be flexible, gracious and balanced in all your considerations.

Are you going to take vacations together? If so, how long and where will it be, who will pay for what and how are you going to travel? You may have a rare family where things can just happen and there is no conflict. Great! But I have had a lot of those "just let it happen" family members in my office to process bitterness over conflicts in expectations.

Define Childcare

Do your kids feel free to leave their children with you anytime night or day? How far in advance do you want to them to "ask" you to watch the grandkids? Do they expect you to feed, bathe, help with homework, or entertain their children? What do they expect you to do about discipline? What foods do they expect you not to give the kids? Do they expect you to be their only babysitter? If your grown child is a single parent, does she expect you to keep the kids so she can work?

You cannot have this discussion too soon. When our four grandchildren were born, it was our joy to be there before, during and after delivery. We helped our daughter with household responsibilities so she could concentrate on the new baby and on recuperating. We asked what she wanted us to do or not do. Linda's mother role-modeled that pattern for us. She came after the delivery of our daughters and took care of the household which allowed Linda to focus on the new baby. Linda's mother clarified before she came that she was there to serve wherever needed and not to just dote on the new grandchild.

A simple principle in grandparenting is to remember who the birth parents are and who has the ultimate responsibility for the grandchildren before God. This also includes who ultimately has the last word regarding the grandchildren. We have devoted chapter ten to explore these issues more in depth.

Clarify Financial Issues

Finances can be as dangerous as a mine field! Can your kids expect loans from you? Do they have to pay them back? Is there interest involved? What are you going to do with your estate if your kids divorce and remarry creating a blended family? If your spouse dies and you marry a mate with children, how will the distribution of the estate change? Do your kids know how that is going to happen? What can your kids expect from you for college tuition, room, board, spending money, cell phone, car insurance, apartment or co-signing for any of the above? Are moral standards or grades a factor? Do they feel you will pay and they will play? Can they finish college and return home and live indefinitely? How much financial support do they expect from you and for how long after school? Bitterness in both the parents and grown kids results when you expect one thing and they expect something quite different.

Are there limits to your "bail-out" policy? Major conflict erupts here when parents fail to come through because the kids believe "you owe it to me" and they expect you to pay, or they reason you have the money to give and don't need it and they do.

If the kids don't go to school or get married, have you clarified how long they can live at home? Should they pay rent or help around the house? Can they stay out as long as they want? Are there house rules and do they have to abide by them? What consequences can they expect if they don't comply? If they divorce, can they move back home? If so, for how long? What are the financial expectations? If a daughter remarries, are you expected to pay for a second wedding? Do you also expect them to bail you out of the consequences of your irresponsible living or spending?

Define Roles

Major hostility can erupt in the area of undefined roles. What are these roles going to look like in real life? Do they expect you to be the "Lone Fixer" for them? Are you going to relate to them on an adult-to-adult basis or parent-to-child basis? Are you ultimately responsible for their happiness or are they for yours?

Have you shifted in your thinking from parenting to mentoring or are you still playing "the parent" role, expecting your grown children to continue to play "the child" role? Do you still expect them to "obey" you as a way of honoring you? Do they expect you to cook their meals or tell them what medications to take and when? Are you supposed to do their laundry and iron their clothes? Do they expect you to help them attain and maintain the same level of lifestyle you have without any struggle?

Stop Mind Reading

One of the three characteristics of a dysfunctional family is that they do not talk. They also are afraid to trust and definitely are not allowed to feel. But the "no talk" rule usually results in mind reading, second guessing and assumption-based relationships. Any or all of these are classic set-ups for conflict and reduced harmony. Often we can guess with a degree of accuracy what they are thinking or how they will react in a given situation. Life experience with them has taught us that. But, in most situations, mind reading or second guessing is a poor basis for any relationship. Even God took the initiative right from the beginning to define our roles, responsibilities and the basis for our relationship with Him (Ex. 20:1-17). Often I hear this dysfunctional statement, "He should know what I need if he loves me." This implies that along with love you also get the gift of omniscience. Our relationship with our kids should mirror our relationship with God. God wanted us to have an intimate relationship with Him so He took the initiative to spell out in scripture how that is to look. Why? Because He knows our ways are totally different from His ways (Isa. 55:8,9).

Jesus clarified to His disciples how to show their love for Him. "If you love Me, you will obey My commandments" (John 14:15). He did *not* say, If you love Me you will feel like it or you will automatically guess what I want and will automatically do it." God even went so far as to define what love is and what love is not (I Cor. 13). He spelled it out to the Corinthian believers who felt that oratory, prophecy, knowledge, faith and understanding mysteries were love. They also believed that martyrdom, sacrifice, and generosity were love. Yes, these can be done out of love, but without love these actions are a waste.

God clearly defines our roles, relationships and responsibilities with Him and each other (John 13:35). Our obedience to Him in these areas defines our fellowship with Him and with one another (I John 1:5-7). His expectations are clear so that we can enjoy each other (I John 1:4). It may be helpful to schedule a family meeting to evaluate your relationship with your kids and determine what adjustments could be made to improve a good relationship.

Let Go of Unlikely Expectations

It is extremely difficult and painful to let go of expectations that are unlikely to materialize.[32] You have to bundle them up in prayer and picture yourself handing them over to God as Abraham willingly handed his son, Isaac, over to God to sacrifice him (Gen. 22). This must be done with the full understanding that it is ultimately His responsibility to determine what He is going to do with your expectations. A miracle may take place. You may see your expectations fulfilled. But on the other hand you may not. Either way, it's His choice (Prov. 3:5,6).

My friends, Brandon and Sherry, visualized their only daughter walking down the aisle in a beautiful white wedding gown. It was their dream. They thought it was Jennifer's dream, too, until that dreaded announcement was made, "Bob and I are living together." There was still hope, but then she got pregnant. Bob then made it clear that he just wanted to be friends, not a husband or a father. He had fathered other children.

As Sherry and Brandon squeezed each other's hand and sobbed in my office, it was plain to see they were grieving the loss of all they hoped, planned and dreamed. They were being forced to go through the pain of breaking through their denial and giving up their hopes. Their task was to bundle up their dreams and deposit them in the loving hands of our Lord. They had to be willing to grieve the loss of the way they hoped things would be and, by the grace of God, accept how things were now. Their response to those changes would determine, in a greater or lesser degree, their own future happiness.

It may seem senseless and totally unfair to have to give up those dreams and expectations. But your relationship with your adult child is likely to improve if you can abandon these dashed hopes, dreams and expectations and begin to appreciate what you have, instead of focusing on what you do not have.[33]

Our children need roots, but they also must have wings if they are to survive on their own. Failure to let them "fly" means you have not completed the second half of your job as parents assigned by God - to let them go (I Cor. 13:11). "Letting go of your expectations of how your children were supposed to turn out means that you may have to accept the reality that you will never have the children you wish you'd had.[34]

It hurts when they choose a different religion or no religion at all. I can still hear the sobs of a pastor's wife as she told how her eighteen-year-old daughter rejected their values and chose to have sex with both older men and teenage boys. This grief mirrors the deep pain God felt over His rebellious adult children, the Israelites. Jeremiah, the weeping prophet, begged and pleaded with Israel's tribe of Judah to return to God.

Your grown kids may choose to live in a different county or state far from you, to remain single, get a divorce or live in an immoral relationship with their significant other. It is a hard reality to accept that the adult child has a right not to live out your expectations, wishes or dreams. Your expectations or your child's may be impossible to fulfill for each other, even if your relationship is a positive one.[35] Expectations must be evaluated and adjusted in every healthy relationship. Now that your children have grown up, your influence is greatly limited.

Grown kids often confide in me that they felt they just couldn't measure up to their parents' unrealistic aspirations for them. They felt they always fell short. The reality is that most adult children who fall short of their parents' expectations are not genuine "fall short" persons. They may be laboring under the burden of parents' inappropriate, overstated, or distorted expectations.[36]

Perfectionist parents can be unhappy with themselves and hang onto the illusion that if they could control people, places or things they would be happy. When they attempt to control people, places and things on the outside, they may be managed by their own fear on the inside. They use their kids as extensions of themselves, living their lives through their children to correct from their own past the feeling that they never measured up. In fact, these parents see their kids' value not for who they but for what they represent to their parents in terms of status or accomplishments.[37]

Trust God When Shattered to the Core

Few shattered dreams can equal the discovery that your adult child is a homosexual or lesbian. Just ask author and popular speaker Barbara Johnson when she discovered her twenty-year-old son was homosexual. She writes, "Finding out about a gay child is agony. It's almost like having a death in the family. But when someone dies you can bury that person and move on with your life. With homosexuality, the pain seems never ending."

Barbara Johnson knows about death first hand. Her eighteen-year-old son joined the Marines and was killed in Vietnam. Just five years later another son died in a head-on collision with a drunk driver. She moved through both of these crises with her emotional health intact. Then she was shattered to the core at the announcement from her third son. "I threw myself down on the bed and a terrible roaring sob burst from me," she relates in her autobiography, *Where Does a Mother Go to Resign?*

"I was alone in the house, and for several terrifying minutes sobs from fear, shock and disbelief shook me. Flashing in my mind was the wonderful son who was so bubbly and happy, such a joy to have around. Thinking of him entwined with some other male, brought heaves of heavy sobbing from deep wounds of agony."[38]

There are five gut-wrenching losses that shatter expectations of a parent of an adult child who is a lesbian or homosexual.[39]

1. The loss of security of a deep abiding lifelong relationship
2. The loss of any source of control of yourself or them
3. The loss of all future dreams (wedding, grandparenting)
4. The loss of reputation as a wife, mother, husband, dad
5. The loss of a relationship that is changed forever

All of these losses call for a change in every expectation of life you have ever had for your kids. They plunge you into a major grief cycle that is worse than death.

First there is the initial shock. Pow! You double up in emotional pain. You can't believe it's true. Your mind throws every weapon of denial against the enemy to no avail. Since denial has failed to protect you, anger erupts. Most anyone or anything can be the target of that anger.

It is not long before you start bargaining with God that you will do anything to stop it, change it or fix it. You make promises to God, yourself, your child, anything to get the pain to end. At this point, you may turn the emotional gun on yourself and begin to blame yourself and conjecture, "If only I would have done this or that, she would not be a lesbian today," or you'll start blaming anyone who had anything to do with your child from birth. Soon the emotion of sadness begins to creep in like a San Francisco fog, slowly rolling in from the Pacific Ocean, engulfing the coastal hills. This sadness is normal. You have suffered a devastating loss.

Then the last phase comes. It doesn't come overnight. It's called acceptance of the reality. This does not mean you feel as good as you did before all this happened. It means you accept the consequences of your loss and choose to live with the loss so you can move on. Like the death of a loved one, in time, the pain does not last as long or go as deep, but it's still there. Now you can live with the loss. Instead of living life looking in the rearview mirror, you can now look out the windshield and only glance in the rearview mirror from time to time.

Barbara Johnson blessed thousands through her life and ministry. Like Jacob of old who wrestled with God and had his hip permanently put out of joint, he could still walk, but he walked with a limp the rest of his life (Gen. 32:25). Barbara ministered with a "limp."

Clarify and Win

No one wants to fail. Most of us do not enjoy conflict. Peace and harmony feel good. Since unfulfilled expectations are one of the biggest contributors to poor relationships, it only stands to reason that discussing mutual expectations should be at the top of your list for an adult-to-adult conversation with your grown kids. No, it is not always easy. Yes, it may be a little awkward, but picture a possible win-win situation. It was unnerving to go to our grown kids and have a family conference and ask if they would share their expectations, but it deepened our relationship with them. Linda and I could not be more proud of our daughters. It certainly feels good to relate with them as adults. But what we have today took work and yes, there is more to come. Now, roll up your sleeves. Go to work. Contact your kids whether married or single. Take the initiative. Ask them if they would be open to share with you their wishes, desires and expectations of you. Then ask permission to share yours. Attempt to negotiate the differences where possible. Clarify now and win.

CHAPTER 4

Points to Ponder

1. Evaluate whether your expectations are "wishes" or "rules."
2. Take the initiative to clarify your mutual expectations on an adult-to-adult level.
3. Ask your grown kids, both married and single, what their expectations are for holidays or special events in advance.
4. Clarify responsibilities before family gatherings.
5. Avoid all attempts to mind read or second guess.
6. Remember who has the ultimate responsibility for your grandchildren.
7. Give all expectations that are unlikely to be fulfilled over to your Heavenly Father.
8. Develop an appreciation for what you have rather than focus on what you have lost.
9. Choose to live your life looking forward and not fixed on the past.
10. Accept full responsibility for your own happiness.
11. Clarify today and win tomorrow.

CHAPTER 4

Clarifying Expectations

Small Group Questions

1. What were your parents' expectations of you and what effect did they have in shaping your life? How did it affect your relationship with them as adults?

2. What expectations did your kids have of you that you did not know about? What expectations did you have of your kids that they did not know about? How did they come to light and how were they handled?

3. Describe an experience of discussing expectations with your grown children in advance of an event. What did you learn about them and them about you? How was this experience beneficial?

4. What misgivings do you have regarding an honest discussion with your adult children about mutual expectations? What would have to change to remove those misgivings?

5. How have your grown children measured up to your expectations? What were they? Why may they not have measured up? What would you do differently now?

6. What expectations have you had to let go? How did you do it? What part did your personal walk with the Lord play in it? What kind of support did you get from friends, family or the church community?

CHAPTER 5

Maintain a Clean Slate

My wife Linda and I can identify with Robert and Bev, the couple I introduced in Chapter one whose daughter had greatly disappointed them. They made mistakes; we made mistakes. Yes, we did the best we could with the information, maturity and wisdom we had at the time we raised our families. But now we have to address the inevitable question, "What do you do now when you realize you made mistakes in the past?" We hurt our kids and they still may be suffering from it today. The good news is that God has specific biblical tools at our disposal to heal any hurt and to rebuild any relationship. Every family will have conflicts and offenses. God has warned us that offenses are inevitable (Luke 17:1). But He also gives us tools to deal with them.

Pause for a moment and ask yourself, "Do I really want a great relationship with my kids?" Then ask yourself a deeper question, "Am I willing to do everything in my own power to make that possible" (Rom. 12:18)? If the answer is "yes," fasten your seat belt because you are in for an incredible ride. The destination? Peace with God, peace with yourself and hopefully, peace with your kids.

Ask God to Search You

Years ago we built a duplex. We lived on one side and our married daughter and family lived on the other side. Something happened there that began to turn my wife, Linda's, relationship around with our daughter. Linda asked if she could tell the story.

For years my (Linda's) relationship with DeeDee was strained and distant. As I began to examine my life more closely in times of prayer, God revealed many ways I had wounded DeeDee's spirit as a child although we were active in full-time ministry all those years. Being a perfectionist, I tried to make her a "perfect" child by correcting every little flaw just like the New Testament Pharisees. I thought my way of doing things was the "right" or "best" way. DeeDee felt like she just couldn't please me. Even in adulthood DeeDee felt she couldn't do anything right to please me.

One day I took my notebook and began to list all the things I did to wound DeeDee's spirit. I was grieved at what God faithfully revealed to me. I knew I needed to share with her how wrong I'd been and ask for forgiveness.

It was early in the day and I knew DeeDee was home alone. I called to see if she was available. As we sat on the couch I began to share what God had been revealing to me about how I raised her and the hurts I caused. With tears flowing I went down my list and told DeeDee how wrong I had been and asked if she would forgive me. And yes, she did. Then something happened I never expected. With the slate wiped clean of my offenses, DeeDee began to open up where she felt she had made some mistakes in her parenting and she shared the struggles she was having as a young mom. If forgiveness is the cornerstone of our relationship with God, it stands to reason it is also the cornerstone of our human relationships, especially with our families (2 Cor. 5:19).

Linda and I both asked God to honestly evaluate our past parenting and even our present manner of relating to our grown kids. King David expressed his need for insight into his past in this way, "Search me, O God, and know my heart; try me and know my anxious thoughts; and see if there be any hurtful way in me, and lead me in the everlasting way" (Ps.139:23-24 NAS).

David's prayer is an honest prayer for all parents. No one is perfect in parenting and our children have suffered in some way because of it. Family and child therapist, Shauna Smith, has said it best, "We have all hurt our children inadvertently, or because we were out of control, or we didn't know better, or because we were trapped in old patterns, or because we thought it was for their own good, or we were afraid of appearing too weak or harsh."[40]

Dr. Larry Stockman has laid out the task before us, "As parents, we must decide whether we are willing to suffer through a confession of our past failings and apologize for them and put them away."[41] Parents who have lost their children by premature death without making attempts to reconcile have been utterly devastated by regret. The past that is not processed is always present. But the past does not need to be the future.

Ask God to share with you any offenses that may have occurred over the years. Don't obsess over it. Just write down what His Spirit reveals. He will be faithful to do this because

He is excited to watch His children use the tools in His Word to restore or increase fellowship with Him and each other.

Address Your Own Objections

There is one thing I can always count on my pride to do, come to my rescue when I don't want to do something I know I should. My pride has a whole library of objections to block any urge I have to obey God. Just thinking about getting and maintaining a clean slate with anyone, especially family, rouses emotional heartburn. But after asking God to reveal issues that are preventing a better relationship with our kids, it is time to remove all the objections to obedience. Evangelist Phil Waldrep lists objections why we may not want to address these issues: "*If we don't talk about it, I'm sure the problem will go away.*"[42]

Denial is not one of God's biblical options in restoring relationships. The past that is not worked through biblically is always present in one form or another. It comes out in many indirect ways. Like an infected wound, it festers and swells until it begins to consume our thoughts and comes through in our actions in subtle ways.

"It's Not All My Fault"

This may be true, but what part of the whole *is* your responsibility? This is no place for "all or nothing" thinking. Scripture is clear, "If possible, so far as it depends on you, be at peace with all men" (Rom. 12:18).

Identify what you did and take full responsibility for it.
"*I didn't mean to hurt anyone.*"

Most of us can honestly say that. It was not the intent of our heart to hurt. We were doing the best with what we had to work with at the time. However, a bullet from friendly fire is just as hurtful as one from an enemy. God required the Israelites to offer sacrifices for unintentional sins (Lev. 4:1-3). Both priest and people had to bring a sin offering if they sinned unintentionally through error.

"Surely they're over it by now."

This is wishful thinking that they have forgotten the hurt. It is a myth that time heals all wounds. The details may fade but the damage remains. For most people, the pain is as fresh as the day it was inflicted.

"I won't ask forgiveness until they apologize to me first."

Out of your kids' own personal pain, they have hurt you. But your waiting until they come to you transfers the responsibility for your obedience over to them. You are only responsible for the things in your circle of responsibility. Scripture is clear, if you know your kids have a grievance towards you, you are responsible to go to them (Matt. 5:23-24).

"I don't know how they will respond."

You are only responsible to God for your obedience, not their response to your obedience. God knows how they will respond, so trust Him for whatever the response may be. If you suffer for doing right, this finds favor with God (I Pet. 2:20). Our success is never defined by the response of others, but only by our obedience to God to do what is right. Any strong objections to obedience must be answered with truth. You will be amazed at the power God will give you to follow through at His direction.

Acknowledge Where You Were Wrong

When *Christianity Today's "Marriage Partnership"* magazine asked me to write an article on forgiveness, I sent them back a proposal simply titled, "Don't Say You're Sorry." Often when a husband says that, his wife responds, "No you're not." He shoots back, "Yes, I am." Then World War III begins.

There is nothing wrong with saying that you're sorry. But I strongly suggest when you talk to your spouse or kids, you say instead, "I was wrong" then attach, "and I am sorry." It is important to say to the offended person the same thing God wants us to say to Him when we offend Him. He tells us to confess our sins or say the same thing He says of them that they are wrong ("confess", lit. "say the same thing"). Most adult children have never heard their parents say the three hardest words in the English language, "I was wrong." They have heard "sorry" or "I apologize," but not the hard words.

The use of these three words has opened more closed doors of relationships than any other words in the English language. Most adult children are yearning for your acknowledgment. Dr. Stockman asserts that there is no better way to convince an adult adolescent that you value him as an equal than to consider him worthy of receiving an apology.[43] It is important to be specific and avoid generalities:

> "I was terribly wrong for sexually abusing you."
>
> "I was wrong for my perfectionist standards you could not measure up to."
>
> "I was wrong for my alcoholism or drug abuse."

> "I was wrong for not supporting you in your sport activities."
>
> "I was wrong for divorcing your mother or father. It was selfish of me."
>
> "I was wrong for being too controlling of you."
>
> "I was wrong for being so critical of you."
>
> "I was wrong for being a workaholic."
>
> "I was wrong for not showing you physical affection and expressing my love for you verbally."
>
> "I was wrong for not praising you."
>
> "I was wrong for disciplining you in anger."
>
> "I was wrong for showing favoritism to your older brother."

Your step of obedience and humility may be used by God to open up your adult children to acknowledge needs in their own life, marriage and parenting. Eventually, they may even be open for some advice.

Be prepared for your adult children to deny that you ever did anything wrong out of a false sense of loyalty. Shauna Smith explains that adult children have a strong loyalty even when parents have been very hurtful. They keep on trying to be good children, fantasizing in their minds that if they are good enough and loyal enough their parents will meet their needs someday.

In extreme cases, grown kids may delude themselves into believing that an abusive parent was just and rational. Unfortunately, one result of this thinking is that the adult child becomes an abuser himself. For the adult child to bury the fact that he was hurt only suppresses the fear, pain and anger and then it is passed on to the next generation.[44]

Avoid a Negative Response

God may lead you in another approach to cleaning the slate from the past. You may be prompted to share with your grown kids that you would like to have a better relationship with them. Ask if they would be open to share with you anything you have done or are doing to prevent that from happening. Here again, Smith warns us not to use any of the following negative responses either when confronted by our children or when they share their hurt at our request.

> Counter attack, "You have no idea how many times you hurt me."
>
> Appeal to your authority, "Is that any way to talk to your parents?"
>
> Get philosophical, "You know, life has its problems."

Defend yourself, "Look, I was under a lot of stress at that time."

Minimize their experience, "It wasn't that bad!"

Accuse them of being ungrateful, "After all we've done for you, you throw this up in our face."

Compare your own past pain, "You haven't gone through half the junk I've been through with you."

Blame shift, "Look who's talking. Have you forgotten all the junk you've done?"

Accuse them of revenge, "You're just trying to hurt us."

Deny the truth, "*That* didn't happen!"

Sarcastic response, "I suppose you never made a mistake."

Super-spiritual, "God still has a lot of work to do in *all* our lives."

Humiliate or shame them, "Look who's talking, Miss Perfect."

Any of these responses are a guaranteed way to end, or greatly reduce, any prospect of a better relationship with your kids. In contrast, a gentle response on your part can remove a potentially tense situation and gently dissolve your kid's anger (Prov. 15:1). This will call for an attitude which reflects some forethought, patience, self-control and a large dose of kindness and understanding. Harsh, hurtful words will only fuel the flames of anger.

Offer to Explain Later

You may feel that if your children only knew what you were dealing with or what the intentions were behind your actions, they would understand and not be so upset. You are probably right. The only decision you have to make is whether you want your explanation heard or you just want to get it off your chest. Asking forgiveness and explaining your actions are two separate functions. Your kids are more open to your explanations *after* you have first acknowledged where you were wrong.

You may have had an extenuating circumstance influencing your past decisions or behavior, but you must avoid explaining it at the time of your confession. Why? They may view your explanation of your wrong behavior as an excuse, instead of a genuine attempt to apologize and to gain understanding.

What should you do if you have legitimate information that would tremendously add to their understanding? Simple, make an offer to explain what was behind it at a later date. For example, "Sometime, now or later, if you are interested, I would be open to explain what was going on when that happened." A statement like this will do a number of things. First, you have made it clear that you understand the difference between forgiveness and understanding. When we confess our sin before God we offer no explanation. We should do the same thing with our kids. "I was wrong" still admits wrong, regardless of the reasons behind it.

Second, you demonstrate your respect for them as adults by letting them decide if and when they want to hear your explanation. As adults they have the right to choose. Third, you demonstrate patience by expressing a willingness to wait until they're ready to listen. If you wait until they're ready, you stand a much better chance not only of being heard but of being understood. The fourth reason that it is beneficial to demonstrate your willingness to wait to share an explanation is their natural curiosity. Now that they are the ones to make that decision, curiosity usually gets the best of them. Often, when the adult children see their parents are not defensive, they want to know what you have to say.

Mending strained relationships may need an extended time of dialog, sharing adult-to-adult with extra energy devoted to listening and understanding. The goal is for healing, not an opportunity to defend oneself, to justify or to exact revenge. Defending is offering an explanation that has not been asked for. Usually it is only our pride that is being defended. Humility and patience would cultivate much richer soil for growth in any relationship.

Accept a Delayed Response

What do you say when your adult child tells you that he is not ready to forgive you now? We could wish everyone practiced the policy of not letting the sun set before their anger has been dealt with (Eph. 4:26). Unfortunately, for most of us the sun has set many times before we were willing to face our anger and forgive the offender. You may say to the reluctant son or daughter that you look forward to the day that they can find it in their heart to forgive you for your sin against them. Express that you are beginning to see just how deeply you have hurt them. Be hopeful and positive. Avoid the prompting to gain revenge by shame-based reactions like, "Just wait till your kids do this to you" or, "If you were a good Christian, you would forgive me."

Remember that reconciliation does not always go easily or quickly. The reality is that it often goes frustratingly slow,[45] but as Dr. Lerner affirms, "Once a relationship is locked into a circular pattern, the whole cycle will change when one person takes the responsibility for changing his or her part in the sequence."[46] Change occurs slowly in close relationships. It takes work. It doesn't occur from hit and run confrontations.[47]

Sadly, some adult children will remain irreconcilable. The Apostle Paul warned his assistant Timothy, that as the end times approach, people will choose to be irreconcilable (2 Tim. 3:3). They may try to use their parents' offenses as an excuse to justify their own wrong behavior or to manipulate their parents. It is our task to refuse to allow the adult child to make us carry the past as his excuse for the present. Adults who have not made peace with their parents before death often carry an enormous burden of regret, guilt and pain the balance of their lives.[48]

Ask for Steps to Rebuild

Decide to rebuild any trust that may have been broken in the past. Ask your adult children if they would begin to consider what you could do to restore or improve your relationship. If you try to guess on your own, you will probably guess wrong and become frustrated.

Many wounded kids are reluctant to forgive because they think they have to automatically trust the one who hurt them. They may be waiting for you to prove you are trustworthy and even test your sincerity to see if you really want to build a relationship based on love and honesty.

Before you criticize their reluctance to automatically open up to you, remember King Solomon wrote that "A brother [adult child] offended is harder to be won than a strong city" (Prov. 18:19 NASB). It may take an enormous effort on your part.

Avoid Guilt-Based Repayment

A word of caution here, avoid all guilt-based efforts to repay your children for the hurt or loss you have caused in the past. Drs. Chapman and Campbell agree that guilt makes parents far less able to deal well with their adult children. Guilt means you are worthy of blame, but if you have confessed your sin to God, you are no longer worthy of blame before Him. If you have confessed your sin to your kids and they refuse to forgive you, you are still guilt free. The Lord Jesus Christ has already paid the full and complete debt for your sin. You are not obligated to pay back your forgiven sins. You are 100% judicially cleared before God (I John 1:9), but it is in your circle of responsibility to make corrections, changes or appropriate restitution to your kids (Rom. 12:18).

Doing penance or paying penalties has rarely worked in the past to restore relationships. Children have a way of using this to manipulate you and even take revenge. Your primary obligation now is to express determination to repair the relationship by acknowledging the wrongs, asking for forgiveness, expressing appropriate sorrow for the events, and making an effort to understand how they felt when you hurt them. They may want to see some appropriate restitution or a change in your behavior or attitude. The process of gaining forgiveness must not be confused with the process of gaining understanding. Forgiveness deals with the "what" question and is granted because of what Christ has done on the cross. Understanding deals with the "why" question and takes time as you share your mutual perspectives of the past in the context of grace, mercy and forgiveness. Attempting to make up for the past only continues the dysfunctional parent-child roles. You are both adults now. You move on from here living out the reality of having been fully forgiven.

Instead of being manipulated by their guilt or yours, take a step back, decide that from this point on you are going to relate to your kids out of appreciation for being forgiven and not from the foolish notion you are going to repay them for the past. In God's eyes your sin is paid in full, whether your kids are willing to acknowledge that or not. Because guilt is such a powerful weapon, it needs to be neutralized through Christ so that you can be led by His Spirit, not by your guilt or theirs. If they put you on a guilt trip, then change travel agents.

Guilt-based relationships are usually poor relationships and tend to be irresponsible ones. You may need to say no to your grown kids for a good reason, but guilt will greatly obscure your judgment and the ability to say no with firmness. If you can't say no because of past guilt, you are still carrying the burdens of the past, and you will contribute to the problem of extended dependency. Do not allow your guilt to ever take away responsibility for what your kids are doing now. If you are acting out of guilt and you telegraph your feelings easily to your kids, they will gladly give up ownership of their problems to you.[49]

It is appropriate to have feelings of sadness for the past. Sadness, sorrow and regret are normal emotions. Even the Apostle Paul never fully got over the fact that he persecuted Christians before he was converted (I Tim. 1:12-16), but his past sins were his present springboard for a whole new appreciation of grace (I Cor. 15:9,10). It also greatly stimulated his love and service for God (2 Cor. 5:14).

After you have acknowledged the past and asked forgiveness of your adult children, you are ready to let it go and replace guilt with healthy love.

Acknowledge and Forgive Their Sin

Our focus revolves around what *we* can do to increase our relationship with our adult children, not what they should do. Often our kids have acted wrongly towards us out of their own woundedness and rebellion. We wish that they would come to us and confess their rebellion, rejection, selfishness, ungratefulness, manipulation, betrayal, disrespect and/or downright disregard for us as parents. That would be nice. But in the real world, that may not happen. Yet what do you do with the hurt they have inflicted?

Take some time to reflect. Ask God to reveal to you all the hurts your children have caused. Don't excuse, minimize or justify their hurtful attitudes and actions, just write them down. Then, go before the Lord in prayer and describe specifically what they did. Avoid all the "understanding" statements of *why* they did it. Just name their sin. Acknowledge to God that you understand it is His responsibility to punish them for their sin and "because of Your death on the cross, I ask you to grant them grace, mercy and pardon just like you have granted to me!" (Eph. 4:32) Conclude with, "I now send my children and their sin over to You and release them to You."

Why send them and their sin to the Lord? The word, "forgive" means to send away ("*apo*" away and "*hiemi*" to send). Those sins were put on Jesus and nailed to the cross (Col. 2:14). You now purpose to be a "sender" and not a "keeper." You are able now to give your adult child the gift of a slate wiped clean by the blood of the Lord Jesus Christ (I John 1:9).

What if they never acknowledge what *they* did? Follow our Lord's example on the cross when He said, "Father forgive them" (Luke 23:24). Those He forgave did not acknowledge their sin or ask to be forgiven. Forgiveness is primarily for the benefit of the one granting it, rather than for the recipient.

The years have passed since Linda and I both cleaned our slate with our older daughter. There is an adult-to-adult respect and openness. We now take vacations together as families. DeeDee and Roger have blessed our ministry financially over the years. She has painted and redecorated our offices and our home. This is the fruit of a clean slate. Linda and I both desire for you to experience a growing relationship with your adult children. It may start with you.

CHAPTER 5

Points to Ponder

1. Determine to improve your relationship at any personal cost.
2. Ask God to reveal to you any offences or hindrances to improving your relationship.
3. Honestly address any of your personal objections to clean the slate.
4. Acknowledge specifically where you were wrong.
5. Avoid responding negatively when your kids confront you or share their hurts.
6. Offer to explain at a later time any reasons behind your past behavior.
7. Patiently wait for their response to your efforts to restore or improve your relationship.
8. Ask for any steps you could take to strengthen or rebuild your relationship.
9. Avoid guilt-based repayment for past wrongs.
10. Separate the issues of forgiveness and understanding in your thinking.

CHAPTER 5

Maintain a Clean Slate

Small Group Questions

1. How did you come to realize there were offenses between you and your grown kids? What part did God's Word and His Spirit play in that understanding? How did God use your kids to bring it to your attention?

2. What has been your experience in cleaning the slate with your kids? What was the offense? How did you approach it? What was their response? What did you learn through that experience?

3. What do you struggle with that prevents you from obeying God? What scriptures have helped you answer your own objections to obedience?

4. What difference does it make to say "I was wrong" or "I'm sorry?" How do you feel when either of these is said to you by someone?

5. What negative response have you received from your parents when you attempted to confront them? What did you do with their response? How has that affected you today?

6. Describe any heart-to-heart talk you have had with your grown kids about your past parenting. How did you approach it? What were you able to explain? What was their response? How has that affected your relationship with them today?

7. What steps have your adult children asked you to take to rebuild or strengthen your relationship with them? How did they share them? What difference has it made?

8. What guilt over your parenting have you had in the past? How did you deal with it? What part did God play in the process? What do you do when guilt feelings return?

9. What have you done with the pain of what your kids have done to hurt you,? If you were able to share forgiveness with your kids, what was their response? What difference did it make to you or them?

10. What has God taught you through giving or receiving forgiveness? What would you suggest others to do or not do based on what you learned?

CHAPTER 6

Develop Emotional Maturity

I've known Kevin for years. He was raised by his mother who never married. He attended a private Christian school, excelling in speech and drama. He was handsome and talented, but at age 21 he demonstrated one small problem. This "small problem" frequently robbed Kevin and his mother of any peace in their home. Why? Kevin was full of rage. In a heated argument, Kevin's mother told him to go get counseling for his rage. That's why he sat across from me one late autumn afternoon. He wanted to know why he could get "set off" so easily and overreact in rage.

I invited Kevin to give himself freedom to feel the anger and in prayer ask God what was the source of that rage. We no more got started in the prayer when he abruptly stopped. "It's my mom," he blurted out, "But I'm not going to blame my mom for my behavior."

Kevin failed to distinguish between excusing behavior and explaining behavior. Excusing behavior is a justification to continue displaying inappropriate behavior. Explaining behavior refers to understanding why we do what we do so that through prayer, forgiveness and understanding, the unacceptable behavioral patterns can be stopped. After clarifying these two issues, he was now able to return to the prayer, asking God to reveal the source of the anger and get it healed.

He began slowly in hushed words. "She made me emotionally dependent on her. It's like she made me responsible for her emotional well-being. I feel like she made me her husband replacement. She went so far as restricting me from having friends my own age while telling me that she was to be my best friend. She even got jealous of any potential girlfriend." His downcast head just moved from side-to-side in what seemed to be both anger and embarrassment. Two words could characterize the long list of his hurts – emotional enmeshment.

Later that year I was speaking at a weekend couples' conference. During the sessions, a woman in her early forties would periodically get up and leave the room and return about ten minutes later. She did this frequently all weekend. Her husband approached me during a break and asked what he could do to get his wife to reduce the frequent calls she was making to her mother who was in good health. "They have to talk … not long, but often, every day. If my wife does not call, her mother will. Her mother gets very angry if my wife doesn't call." The same two words describe it all - emotional enmeshment.

What could Kevin's mother or the mother of the frequent caller do to end this emotional enmeshment that is robbing all parties concerned of a better quality of life in Christ?

Assume Responsibility for Your own Emotional Maturity

It is evident that Kevin and our frequent caller friend were given the unhealthy responsibility by their parents to meet their ultimate emotional needs. Some refer to this practice as "emotional incest." Dr. John Friel compares this emotional enmeshment to tangled fishing lines. It is nearly impossible for enmeshed parents and grown children to see where their identities end and the other's identity begins. The parents' problems are the kids' problems. The kids blame the parents for their unhappiness and the parents blame the kids. No one can make a move without the other person knowing about it or commenting on it. Everyone is into everyone else's business. No one takes responsibility for their own lives.[50] It is as if the parent has an empty emotional bucket and the adult children are given the responsibility to fill it, and re-fill it frequently. The very first step towards ending this pattern is to acknowledge to yourself that you and you alone are responsible before God for your own emotional maturity.

Dr. James Friesen expressed it this way, "While God is certainly instrumental in guiding and blessing our maturation, it is our job, bestowed upon us way back in the garden, to mature. Maturity is not a spiritual gift, nor a by-product of salvation. It is something we, as Christians, must work on our entire lives."[51] But if you fail to grow up emotionally yourself, you may use your grown kids to meet your own un-met needs. This will certainly result in resentment in them toward you. The Apostle Paul made it clear whose responsibility it was to grow up. "When I was a child, I used to speak like a child, think like a child, reason like a child; when I became a man, I did away with childish things" (I Cor. 13:11).

Notice four times Paul used the pronoun, "I." Nowhere in that verse did he use "they," "them," or "you." When he became an adult he took full responsibility to end the childish need to emotionally cling to anyone. As an adult, he took full, personal responsibility for himself and he did away with all immature forms of conversation, behavior and thinking. The Greek word "k*atargeo*" which we translate "did away with" means "to put away, to render non-operative, powerless; remove the meaning and significance from; to cause a person to be free from something that has been binding him, to break the hold, finish it off, to be done with it."

"*Katargeo*" is a strong verb. It certainly involves a great effort and struggle. Childish ways do not just fall away as leaves off a tree. For Kevin's mom to stand up straight with resolve and declare to herself, "I, not Kevin, am totally responsible for my own emotional maturity and stability" would be hard. After all these years of dependency, it would take a stomach wrenching effort on her part to do that.

Your enmeshed grown kids will also struggle to end their dependence on you. They may feel uncomfortable, disloyal, dishonoring, selfish, even deserving to be punished. They may need your help to put away their childish ways of thinking and actions. How? Stop rewarding their efforts to remain dependent on you by encouraging them to live with you when they are financially able to live on their own. Refuse to bail them out financially when they foolishly spend their own resources. Make them think through their own problems first, before you offer your input.

Replace the Lie with the Truth

Why do we use our grown kids to fill our own emotional buckets? Simple, we may have a core belief of the heart that if we do not stay inordinately connected, we will be alone, not needed or worse yet, abandoned. This is not an adult emotion. Usually, there is a deep wound in the parent's developmental years that inserted the lie that they *are* alone even though as an adult they know all the verses indicating that God will never leave them or abandon them (Heb. 13:5).

If the truth were known, parents who are still emotionally enmeshed have made one adult (their grown kid) to act in the place of God on their behalf. Enmeshment is a God substitute relationship. God is removed from life's picture as it relates to emotional security. In reality, the parent is the adult child's idol and the child is the parent's idol.

Parents can be very religious outwardly, but secretly, they have substituted another person in the role that only God should have. Eli, an Old Testament priest, is a classic example of being outwardly religious but secretly dependent. He failed to rebuke his two grown sons, who were also priests, for their gross immorality with the women who came to the tabernacle to offer sacrifices. Why did Eli not put a stop to this vile behavior? In his heart, he honored his grown kids more than the God he was supposed to be serving (I Sam. 2:29; 3:13). As a result of his enmeshment with his sons and his failure to restrain them, God allowed the Philistines to kill the sons, then, He removed Eli's family from the priesthood over the next three generations.

Kevin's mother took him with her to church every time the church doors were opened. She even put him in a conservative Christian school. Outwardly, she was deeply Christian; inwardly, she was deeply enmeshed. God takes a very dim view of this pattern. The Lord Jesus clearly declared, "He who loves father or mother more than Me is not worthy of

Me and he who loves son or daughter more than Me is not worthy of Me" (Matt. 10:37 NASV).

No one on this planet is responsible for your emotional stability but you and you alone. God and God alone can fill your empty bucket by the filling of His Holy Spirit (Eph. 5:18). Only God has promised to become a wellspring inside, filling you from the inside out, not the outside in with adult children relationships (John 4:14). Your task is to resist any temptation to get your unmet emotional needs met through your adult children. Do not ask your kids to fill emotional needs that you can't meet on your own.

Release Your Children

The only thing worse than a mistake, is an uncorrected mistake. Earlier I stated that I believe you did the best job you could have done with the information and maturity you had at the time. Now you are choosing to put away, once and for all, your habit of making your kids responsible to make you feel good and secure. That is your responsibility with God inside you, growing you to maturity (Phil. 1:6; 2:13). Release your children from the responsibility for your ultimate happiness and emotional security.

You may need to confess your sin of selfishness for using them and making them responsible for your happiness, which is a form of idolatry. Affirm that you are now assuming that responsibility and are going to relate to them on an adult-to-adult basis while purposing to deepen your own relationship with God. How?

Remind yourself that the second fruit of the Holy Spirit is "joy" (Gal. 5:22). Then, change your core belief system from depending on your kids to fill your emotional bucket to allowing God to fill you with the Holy Spirit (Eph. 5:15-21). This step will free you to establish healthy relationships with them, not out of neediness, but out of contentment. You are now free to let each person in your family be accountable for his/her own happiness. Your feelings are your own responsibility. They are no one else's job but your own.

Inform your grown kids that you are going to stop all attempts to rebuild or fix your own past personal life through parenting. Kevin's mom had experienced many emotionally abandoning events in her developmental years. Her fear of re-experiencing those frightful emotions motivated her to assign Kevin the responsibility to make her secure in adulthood. Later, to her credit, she did seek appropriate counsel to heal the emotional hurts of the past that were controlling her present. The past that is not processed biblically is always present and shows up most keenly in close relationships.

Inform them that you are not going to use them as your confessor and confidant any longer. You will instead seek Christian peers or your pastor to share things that are not appropriate to share with the kids, such as the intimate needs in your marriage relationship. If you have made them your best friend, you may have failed to build meaningful relationships with your peers, especially in the body of Christ, God's new family. God has designed a whole new family system, the church, that transcends the human family, including our kids (I Cor. 12:12-27).

Jesus shocked the multitudes and His followers when his mother and siblings sought to speak with Him. They may have wanted to attach themselves to Him now (for His brothers did not believe in Him earlier, John 7:5) and receive some special favor through family ties. When informed of His family's request, He responded to the messenger, "Who is My mother and who are My brothers?" Stretching out His hand toward a large group of men and women, He said, "Here are My mother and My brothers!" Then he concluded, "For whoever does the will of My Father in heaven is My brother and sister and mother" (Matt. 12:46-50). Jesus radically re-defined family relations. Welcome to your new family.

By releasing your grown kids from the responsibility to meet your emotional needs, it frees you to seek those things which are above where Christ is, instead of setting your mind on things on the earth where your kids live (Col. 3:1-2). Why? "For you died, and your life is hidden with Christ in God" (vs. 3).

Break Off Unhealthy Dependent Patterns

Earlier in the chapter, I mentioned a lady who had to call her mother often. When she was a child, her parents divorced and she was raised by her mom. This is one of the common unhealthy patterns in the mom-daughter relationship as a result of a divorce. The nurturing roles get reversed. The very thing that the daughter needed from her mother, her mother asked the child to give to her. Why? Often the divorcee adult will cling to the child for emotional support. One result of this is that it gives the child a false sense of empowerment and importance. This dysfunctional pattern quickly robs a child of her childhood. The frequent caller daughter reported that she felt she never had a childhood and that she had to be the parent. One of the tragic results was that the grown daughter was now over-responsible for everything because of the child-like lie instilled by her mother that she *was* responsible for everything. The daughter willingly fulfilled three major family functions. The daughter had to provide some or all of the structures (adult roles), the stability (emotional) and security (mediator and adult responsibilities).[52] Mom did everything she could to discourage her daughter to grow up so that she would be dependent on her mom. The mother became a "nesting parent". The mother bird is going to stay in the nest the rest of her life *with* her chicks.[53]

Why did the "nesting mom" get angry with the daughter if she failed to call her? Simple, when the mom felt alone and her daughter did not call, fear kicked in. Then mom shifted from fear to anger because the daughter failed to prevent her from feeling fearful, an emotion she hated. So when the daughter returned her mother's call, she was met with anger, not love and appreciation. This unhealthy pattern is called a fear bond, not a love bond. Fear bonds in relationships are formed around attempts to avoid negative feelings or pain. The bond between the frequent callers was a fear bond. The daughter was responsible to keep her mother from feeling fear of rejection, abandonment, shame and guilt. Love bonds, by contrast, motivate each person to live in love, truth, openness, closeness, joy, peace and a balance of give and take.[54]

The Apostle John explains that mature love removes fear in a relationship (I John 4:18). But the opposite can also be true, strong fear pushes away feelings of love. The bond that kept both of the frequent callers connected was mutual fear of being alone. What should the mother do to break these unhealthy patterns of dependence within herself?

Stop Relating to Your Adult children as Kids

Stop playing the "I-am-the-parent, you-are-the-child" game. How? Change your core belief of viewing your grown child as a kid and view them as an adult. Remember, for the adult child to "play child," someone must play the parent part.[55] Recognize that as a parent, you have matured but you may have failed to let your relationship with your adult child mature as he became an adult. The frequent caller mom still viewed her daughter as a child who needed to obey her to keep her from feeling afraid. That is why the daughter was greeted with anger for failing to call because she was not there to rescue mom from her fears.

Stop Confusing "Closeness" with "Sameness"

One of the hallmarks of emotional maturity is to recognize the validity of multiple differences: to understand that people think, feel and react differently. Some family members are especially prone to have as their core belief that theirs is the only "reality" that should be agreed upon by all.[56]

The frequent caller daughter felt mentally trapped because she was not allowed to have separate thoughts from her mother. Why? Mom believed she was only close if they each felt and thought alike. Mom could cut the emotional ties that bound them together by allowing her grown daughter to have her own thoughts and opinions that were different from hers. The mother's fear that independent thoughts meant distance fed her fear of abandonment.

One of the root issues of both Kevin's mother and the frequent caller's mom is the role of being a nurturer and this feeling of being needed can be addictive.[57] Most addictions are designed to change our moods. Both of these moms altered their moods through their grown kids. When they felt the emotion of loneliness, they would go to their adult children for an emotional fix to numb the negative emotion. It stopped them from feeling that negative feeling. Again, mood altering is not wrong if it is done by the Holy Spirit (Eph. 5:18-21). Instead of going to a grown child for a "fix," go to God in a prayer. Ask Him to fill that void or identify the source of the fear that is driving your need for a relational fix (Phil. 4:6, 7).

Develop Outside Interests

Dependent parents need to take the initiative to develop other interests. Enmeshment may have happened because parents failed to develop other interests as their children reached physical maturity. It may take a step of faith out of the comfort zone of fear for a parent to explore the wealth of things they can do that is not related to their kids. Fear restricts but faith expands.

The last words of our Lord to His followers were to go and make disciples of all nations (Matt. 28:19-20). That commission alone offers different possibilities. Are you physically impaired? We are guardians of a 78 year old bedfast widow with Parkinson's disease who has several notebooks of prayer journals. She actively prays for hundreds of people and keeps in touch with many of them. We visit her often and listen to story after story of answered prayer and reports from the mission field. She has said often that she does not have time to feel sorry for herself because she has so much to do.

Valerie Wiener really puts this into perspective when she says, "The parents who often serve as the best role models for independent adult children are those who have a strong sense of individuality, who do not wait on their children, who do not measure themselves by the success or failure of their children, live their own lives and let their grown children do the same. They live complete lives themselves, setting a positive example for their children."[58]

Stop Frequent Intrusions

Another pattern that needs to end is frequent intrusive contact in your kids' lives. If there is a major illness, surgery or accident, frequent updates are appropriate, but not calling to get an emotional fix.

The Apostle Paul urged the Roman believers not to provide an occasion to fulfill the lust of the flesh (Rom. 13:14). The same principle applies here. Don't grab your phone to get a fleshly, emotional fix. You may react and say you can't help yourself. That feeling is a lie that has been rooted deep in your core belief system. You can do anything that God expects from you through Jesus Christ our Lord (Phil. 4:13). Your need is God's opportunity. He loves people with needs (Rev. 3:14-18). It hurts Him when we turn to god replacements to get those needs met.

Respect Their Time

Choose to respect your adult kids' time. Families, especially those with children at home, are very busy. They are a priority. It does not mean they should not be available to you, but your kids are not your emotional ATM machine, ready to dispense an emotional fix on call 24/7. This is not a love issue. Your kids probably love you but are also busy with their own lives. Have an adult-to-adult conversation with them and inquire when it would work for them to call you or you call them. That mutual respect for each others' time will go a long way toward improving your relationship. The husband of the frequent caller indicated they had no private time as a couple because her mother failed repeatedly to respect any of their time.

Avoid Guilt Trips

Avoid at all costs the guilt trip calls. "Why haven't you called me today?" Or the shaming call, "You know I'm just your mother." Then there are the "poor me" calls. "I guess you're too busy to talk to your poor old mother." These kinds of statements do not bring closeness; they really fuel a greater desire for distance from you.

Slay the Monster of Fear

If you were to ask Kevin what is the one word that characterizes his mother's relationship with him, guess what he would say? If you thought "control," you got it! We have alluded to it often in this chapter. The word, control, fully depicts an adult-to-child relationship where the parent is emotionally unhealthy and very dependent and needy. Kevin's mom attempted to control every facet of his life. Why? Because any action, thought or word that hinted of "not being there for her" 24/7 was met by either anger, manipulation, guilt trips, shaming or threats of some form of revenge.

Controllers rarely feel loved. Why? Because they know down deep that the only reason people spend time with them is because they are manipulating them. If they stopped threatening or manipulating, they would be abandoned. No healthy person interprets control as love but as rejection.

To Kevin's credit, he now sees it for what it is and has stopped rewarding his mom's efforts to continue by his compliance. He has his own home and career and is now married. Does he still love his mom? Yes! Does he reward her efforts to control? No! But he does so respectfully. Part of living a happy life is being able to let go of the uncontrollable. His mom has her own task. There is a monster of fear that has been managing her life. This fear of being alone has overpowered everything she knows to be right. Confidentially, she would say she is embarrassed. What should she do?

Feel the Fear

The first step is the one we took Kevin through to discover the object of his anger. For his mother's part, it is not anger as much as fear. Remember, control does not come from faith or trust. Control comes from fear, usually the fear of failure or abandonment.

So, her first step is to give herself permission to feel the emotion of fear just like the Psalmist allowed himself to acknowledge his despair. He felt depressed but he did not beat himself up for it. He allowed himself to feel it and then asked himself where those emotions were coming from. "Why are you cast down, O my soul? Why are you disquieted within me?" (Psalm 42:5a). By asking that question, he discovered he had lost hope in God and now he had something tangible to deal with. This discovery came as a result of feeling the emotion, then following it down to the need. In the case of anger, Dr. Les Carter says, "Anger is an emotion that speaks up for personal needs."[59] I would say the same thing of fear: it has an object and it, too, reveals a need.

Reveal the Source

The second thing I would suggest for Kevin's mom or any controlling parent is to ask God in a time of prayer to reveal the source of that fear. There are usually two sources. The first are historical events. Emotions come from thoughts and the thoughts may come from events, especially from the early developmental years. It could come from childhood abuse, either physically or emotionally. One may say to himself, "I was not in control so I got hurt. Now I am going to be in control and will not get hurt again."

Other historical events as a source of fear could be the death or divorce of parents or being rejected, abandoned, left out, ignored or just tolerated. A parent can be afraid of failing as a parent so he controls everything to prevent the child from embarrassing him or invalidating him as a perfect parent.

Forgive Offenders

If the fear of being alone came from an abandoning parent or one who was there physically *but* not emotionally, you would name their sin before the Lord in prayer and describe how it affected you, then send the offender and their sin over to the Lord Jesus Christ. Remember, the Greek word, forgive (*aphiemi*), means to send away, not to release. Your job is to send them over to Jesus and then release them and walk away. You are then free.

Detect the Lie

The second source of fear is the *lie* that gets injected into the heart as a result of a hurtful event. My father abandoned my family when I was a kid. That was the event. The meaning I put on that event was that I must not be loved. The lie that was then injected into my core belief system was that I was not loveable. The events of my dad's abandonment slipped into the back of my mind. The lie went straight to my heart and became a managing emotion. Kevin's mom also needed to forgive her dad and mom for their parenting that hurt her. Then, she needed to look for the lie that she is alone and needs Kevin as her adult security blanket.

Reveal the Truth

In a prayer, Kevin's mom could acknowledge that she believes that she is alone or would be rejected if she made a mistake, then ask God to reveal the truth to her. He may do it directly through His Word or by another believer speaking God's truth to her. Either way, she needs to allow God to speak truth to her heart and she needs to reject the lie for what it is and replace it with the truth.

Kiss the Monster Good Bye

That monster of fear will greatly diminish if not fade away. What's left? The habits of control. They need to be identified, renounced and repented of, then, replaced with healthy relational patterns. What will be the result? First, personal power and control would return to her life. She would now be able to be led by the Hoy Spirit and not the negative feelings of fear.

Next, she could enjoy her son on an adult-to-adult basis. They both can appreciate each others' gifts and talents instead of looking for ways to manipulate each other for emotional validation. A new source of energy would come. Instead of an emotional drain of fear all day, there would be restored energy to enjoy all day. There would be a deepening relationship with God as He is restored to His rightful place as the center of her life rather than her former god replacement - her son.

Now she can get a life. She can now live out God's destiny for her life. "For those who are led by the Spirit of the Lord are the sons of God" (Rom. 8:14). Instead of being led by fear, she now can be led by faith. Yes, this will be scary at first, but taking baby steps of faith will result in giant leaps toward maturity. She will now be able to enjoy new friendships. She can even be a friend now instead of a needy "taker" who sucks the emotional energy out of others.

It wasn't too many years after Kevin's initial visit that I received a wedding invitation from him. What a wedding! He is a policeman now. He is a man. And mom has a life. Are there struggles? Yes. It has not been easy for either of them. One relationship ended, parent-to-child. Today it is adult-to-adult and mom is emotionally free.

CHAPTER 6

Points to Ponder

1. Assume full responsibility for your own emotional health.
2. Put away your child-like perspective.
3. Replace the lies you have believed with the truth.
4. Release your children from the responsibility for your ultimate happiness.
5. Choose to be filled with the Holy Spirit.
6. Break off unhealthy patterns of dependency.
7. Resist relating to your adult children as kids.
8. Stop confusing "closeness" with "sameness."
9. Develop outside interests.
10. Stop frequent intrusions by respecting their time.
11. Avoid guilt and shame trips.
12. Slay the monster of fear by facing it head on by faith.

CHAPTER 6

Develop Emotional Maturity

Small Group Questions

1. What patterns of dependency have you observed in yourself or someone close to you?

2. Why do you think parents may not want to assume responsibility for their own emotional maturity?

3. What was the most difficult habit you had to break in order to completely free yourself from your adult child?

4. What were some of the lies you believed about yourself that prevented you from being emotionally free in adulthood?

5. What steps have you taken or do you need to take to fully release your grown kids from the responsibility for your happiness?

6. How have you observed the confusion of "closeness" and "sameness" pattern in relationships?

7. What outside interests have you developed apart from your kids?

8. In what ways have you demonstrated respect for your kids' time?

9. What experience have you had of others attempting to put you on a guilt or shame trip? How did it feel? What was your response?

10. What were points of fear you had to face in releasing your grown kids? How did you do it? What was their response? What struggles do you have today? How can the group pray for you?

CHAPTER 7

Love and Respect Them

DeeDee was a beautiful bride. Roger was a handsome groom. Linda and I were thrilled to celebrate our daughter's marriage to Roger. A dad could not be more proud than I was of my daughter. Because Roger's dad was also a pastor, we both did the honors of performing the ceremony. Of course, I walked her down the aisle first.

There was something the eye of my imagination caught that no one in the audience saw. DeeDee was carrying an imaginary red bucket. As Roger filed in with his groomsmen, I saw the same thing. He was carrying an imaginary red bucket. There were white labels on each of them with black lettering. The label on DeeDee's bucket said, "Love" and on Roger's, "Respect."

Although the following words were never said, I could hear in my mind, Roger's dad say to me, "Who has had the responsibility to fill DeeDee's love bucket?" I would answer, "For 21 years Linda and I have had the responsibility to fill DeeDee's love bucket. Today we transfer that responsibility over to Roger." I would kiss DeeDee on the cheek and give her to Roger as he stepped forward. As I now stood next to Roger's dad in front of this lovely couple, I would then ask, "Who has had the responsibility to fill Roger's respect bucket?" His dad would say, "Roger's mother and I have had the responsibility to fill Roger's respect bucket, but today we transfer that responsibility over to DeeDee." The service concluded and we all enjoyed a lovely reception. Our job was done. Or so we thought.

Love and Respect for Life

In one part of the wedding ceremony, I turned to DeeDee and said, "Today ends a relationship that your mother and I have had with you for 21 years." Then I hastened on to say, "But today begins a new relationship with you that we look forward to enjoying the rest of our lives." Although we let our daughter go so that she could "leave and cleave" (Gen. 2:24), there were two very important things that did not change. We are still responsible to do our part to continue to love and respect both DeeDee and Roger. Our roles have changed, but it was a gradual transition as she grew up. Our responsibility to demonstrate love and respect is a permanent privilege and obligation. The *ways* they are expressed on an adult-to-adult level now may need to be modified, but the essence of the love and respect does not change at all.

Adjust Your Approach

Whether your grown children are single or married, it is your responsibility to learn how to express your love and respect on an adult-to-adult level. What was appropriate at age 6 is different at age 26. How your son felt respected at age 10 is considerably different at age 40. Conflict can arise when the symbols of love and respect are not adjusted to be age appropriate.

When our girls were little, out of our love for them, they had to be managed and corrected appropriately. God connects love with appropriate discipline and instruction, "For whom the Lord loves He chastens" (Heb. 12:6a). He goes on to explain that all His children are disciplined when needed just like an earthly parent has to correct wrong behavior (vs. 9). Now that our kids are adults all that changes. Our means of expressing our love and respect must adjust also.

Realize They are Different than You

It is important for you to understand that what makes you feel loved may not make your adult children feel loved. Communication can break down and unintentional conflict can arise when people have different symbols of the same concepts – like love.[60] It is understandable that when we, as parents, want to express our love, we use our own symbols in expressing love rather than our kids' symbols to demonstrate caring.

Dr. Gary Chapman's excellent book, *The Five Love Languages* equals "symbols" with "love languages." Chapman explains that research has identified at least five common symbols or languages of love that are found in most cultures. Simply stated they are: words of affirmation, quality time, receiving gifts, acts of service and physical touch. What is important here is to acknowledge that your grown children may have different symbols of what it means to be loved and respected than you do. To love them from your perspective is at least naïve on one hand and insensitive on the other. True, you are their parents and they have your genes, but it is your responsibility to understand that God has uniquely designed them to be different. It is your task to identify those differences and relate to them fully acknowledging their differences.

It was an eye opener for us to learn the love symbols of our grown daughters. During Michelle's growing up years, she continually made gifts for people in very special and creative ways. She would even use the money she received from family and friends to buy or make gifts for others. Her symbol of love is giving and receiving thoughtful gifts.

When Michelle celebrated her 25th birthday, she lived 600 miles away and was supporting herself, so we thought we would send a gift of money instead of purchasing a gift. She received other monetary gifts as well. However, a friend bought her a little gift and she nearly cried and said, "This gift is really special." It was the only one she received that she could open. When Linda and I heard this we looked at each other and thought, "Oh." Yes, she appreciated the thoughtfulness of each of us and she genuinely showed it. But after 25 years we did not know that she loves to open gifts. This makes her feel extra special. She is different from us. It is our responsibility to inquire of our grown daughters what makes them feel loved.

If we, as parents, fail to know and understand our grown kids' symbols of love and care, we may get a negative response from our attempts to express love and be left clueless. Why? It is not that our intentions were wrong but that we did not realize their symbols are different than ours. We think we're giving our grown kids what they need or want while they may have a totally different idea. We plan for success but sometimes to our surprise we find failure staring us in the face.

Discover Their Love and Respect Symbols

Dr. Chapman believes, in no uncertain terms, that it is the parents' job to know the primary love language of their adult children and to give heavy doses of love in this language.[61]

But finding out what says, "I love you" may not be that easy. Some parents have asked their kids to finish the simple statement, "I feel loved when … and I feel unloved when. …" But what some have heard back are statements like:

- "Why are you asking me now?" (implying they didn't feel loved in the past).
- "If I have to tell you, it wouldn't mean much to me" (implying you should be mind readers).
- "You should just know because you are my parents" (implying that parents are endowed with the quality of omniscience).

Although each of these negative responses reflect some dysfunctional thinking on the part of the adult kids, the parent should still go the extra mile to encourage them to share what says, "I love you." Do not allow their negative responses to deter you and *at all costs* do not defend yourself for the past. Have that discussion at a later time. Keep your heart sensitive and reassure them of your love and your desire to express it in ways that are meaningful to them.

Express Verbal Compliments

Verbal expressions of accomplishment are not only appropriate but are biblical. King Solomon declared, "Let another man praise you and not your own mouth" (Prov. 27:2a). It is easy to confuse bragging about yourself, which is motivated by pride, with allowing another to express affirmation or praise for your great efforts. Allowing another to give you appropriate praise can be a little humbling, too. You may have a son or daughter who is wired by God to feel genuinely loved when he/she hears sincere praise.

My wife, Linda, shared to me one evening, "I live on your words of praise and appreciation." My initial thought was that's what I hear in counseling when I sense someone is seeking approval through performance. Yes, sometimes that's the case. But for one who has been programmed by God to feel love through praise, it's a totally different matter. For the record, God even praised His own Son (Luke 3:22).

All kids appreciate sincere praise from time to time, but for many, praise is their primary symbol of love. It is our task to look for opportunities to express verbal compliments, if for no other reason than to be a consistent source of encouragement. Guys want to hear verbal compliments about their jobs, cars, trucks, homes, landscaping, parenting, husband roles, financial management, church involvement, spiritual depth and godly character. Be duly warned, men and sons primarily translate the five symbols of love through respect. If your son has to choose between love and respect, he will choose respect hands down.

Daughters really love to hear how nice they look, love their husbands, care for the family, manage schedules, balance work and home, shop wisely and have a gracious and godly spirit. For further suggestions, read Proverbs 31 to see if there are other qualities in your daughter that parallel the virtuous woman described there.

Express Love through Respect

If my wife lives on the words I express, then I would have to admit that I feel most loved when she demonstrates respect for me. Your son will feel the same way. And just how can you show it? Respect his judgment. He may not be batting 1,000 in this department but find something you can affirm regarding his judgment. Acknowledge your respect for his knowledge. It may not be in areas you are familiar with, but even if it is, demonstrate respect for it. This also includes his opinions. You may have a different opinion, but be sure to respect his. It would not hurt at all if on occasions you even demonstrated deference to him and his choices.

Respect his abilities which may mean you allow him to figure some things out on his own. What is important is to convey that you believe in your grown son. Whether it is his primary symbol of love or not, your son needs to hear you verbally affirm his competency in some area. But, avoid like the plague, all expressions of sarcasm and mocking. If you want distance, this will do it. If you feel you want to offer constructive criticism, share it *privately* and avoid any and all put downs. Publicly, do all you can to demonstrate support and respect. Any way you slice it, verbal affirmation for your son is everything, regardless of his other symbols of love.

Spend Quality Time

It was a quiet evening at my oldest daughter's home and all the grandkids were in bed. The topic came up of what makes us feel loved. Reflecting deeply, DeeDee shared that she felt most loved when a person spends time with her.

I will never forget that night. So many things all of a sudden made sense. I recall how she shared with us how hurt she was when we did not come over to their apartment when they first got married. Remember, Linda and I were counseled to wait until they invited us. We waited and waited. Then, out of hurt, she asked why we never came over to visit them and see their new apartment. Yes, our mistake was unintentional, but it hurt none the less. Quality time that expressed our undivided attention is what said, "I love you" to her. For all those weeks our absence was unintentionally saying to her, "We don't love you."

As I sat in the recliner that evening at her home, my mind went through the countless times we took care of the grandkids, praised her for her incredible decorating skills, bought her thoughtful little gifts from around the world where we trained biblical counselors on five continents. We even brought back gifts for all four of the grandkids.

My heart sank. How I wished I had known this years ago. I am sure she knew we loved her. But I thought to myself, "How many times did I focus my attention on just her? How many times did I give a part of me and not just thoughtful gifts or heroic sacrificial efforts? Yes, we experienced many activities and interactions together through the years. But when was the last time it was an activity planned for the purpose of being together?"

While writing this chapter, my mind went back about six months ago, when I took her out to a lovely dinner and afterwards walked around the Kansas City Plaza and window shopped through several stores. What a terrific evening we both felt it was! We didn't discuss kids, spouses, work, church, vacations or problems; we just enjoyed each other. I am embarrassed to say I have not made this a regular event. The words of Drs. Campbell and Chapman were really convicting to me. "For parents who realize that they have a distant relationship with their adult children, a change in lifestyle is called for. You can no longer do what you have always done if you minimize the weakness of this parenting style. If your problem is that you are too busy working or helping others, you need to slow down and begin connecting with your children.[62]

I personally believe this is why God requires a church to select a pastor who has an excellent track record at home (I Tim. 3:4,5). Why? Because ministry is all about caring both at church and at home! And caring at home may mean focused time with the kids who define love by spending quality time with them. Then, keep it up when that child becomes an adult. The concept of "leave and cleave" in marriage does not mean an end to their need for some of your attention, but adjust it to fit your new roles and schedules.

Share Thoughtful Gifts

Linda and I have the privilege of responding to invitations all over the world to come and train leaders how to help their people work through problems in living from scripture. This calling has taken us to Asia, Africa, Europe, North and South America, Central America and the West Indies. From the time our plane leaves Kansas City, Missouri, our minds are on two things. First, preparation and anticipation of the teaching and training we are about to do. Second, how can we find a unique gift from that country for each of our family members?

Special and unique, but not costly gifts would be a way to express love to Michelle'. When it is either sent to her or given in person, our daughter's enthusiasm is like a little kid. It's not the gift in and of itself, but it says, "You were thinking of me while you were 'saving the world.' I'm in your thoughts and you haven't forgotten me with everything else you had on your mind." All of us deeply appreciate when someone thinks of us and expresses it in a verbal or tangible way. To those who love gifts as an expression of love, it boldly says, "You thought of me. You had to think of me to purchase that gift."

Recently Linda and I were teaching in China. To this day, I remember walking through many Chinese shopping areas scouring for a unique gift for Michelle. What a delight it was to find beautiful silk robes for her and her (then) fiancé, Greg. Relief? Yes! It was not an obligation on our part but a tangible way to tell our 25-year-old daughter, "We love you." Yes, we purchased gifts for the rest of the family, too.

If receiving gifts is your adult child's symbol of love, the gift for him does not have to be an expensive set of golf clubs or a beautiful diamond. It is *not* about the cost; it is the symbol that you really thought of them. For the gift receiver, it is not just the thought that counts; it's the special effort of acquiring the gift and giving it as an expression of your love. It is a symbol of love. Plus, it will probably mean more to them than to you.

Love in Deed and in Truth

Of all the symbols of love, thoughtful acts of service are probably the most prominent one. How often I have heard in the counseling room when an adult child searches for evidence of being loved by their parents, they explain all the things their parents did for them. They may not have shown their love verbally ("I love you") or physically (hugs), but they put a roof over their heads, food in their tummies and clothes on their backs and this was their translation of love. This is usually the mindset of an older generation. Unfortunately, this has been hurtful to some, primarily when there was a failure on the adult's part to bond with their child physically and emotionally during their developmental years. That is one side of the coin. There is another side.

Some adult children feel especially loved if you do things for them that they would like you to do. For the most part, these are very practical requests. Here is where you really need to be on your toes. These are not practical things that are necessarily important to you. It is important that you ask them what practical projects you could do that would say to them, "I love you/" Whatever you do, don't guess. Why? You could pour a lot of time and effort into something they did not need or that they wanted to do themselves or had planned to have taken care of another way. Your efforts appear to be wasted by their lack of appreciation and you may interpret it as ungratefulness.

Wanda and Frank were invited over for Sunday dinner at their daughter's home. Wanda was raised on a mid-west farm with five siblings. All meal times were a team effort. Everyone pitched in. Yes, Karen loved her mother but dreaded having her over for a meal. Why? When mom walked in, she took over just like on the farm. You didn't need to be told, you knew what needed to be done and you just did it. When

Wanda saw the unpeeled potatoes on the counter she started peeling. Karen didn't want them peeled; she wanted to try a new recipe that involved leaving the potato skins on. Wanda grabbed a large pan to boil water in for iced tea. When Karen discovered it, she smiled faintly while glancing out on the sun porch at the gallon jar of sun tea she had set out to brew. It gets worse.

Karen asked if her mom would take two-year-old Megan and three-year-old Brandon out of the kitchen and play with them. Wanda quietly dismissed the request stating that they didn't bother her and turned to start snapping the garden fresh string beans. Wanda happened to comment to Frank on the way home how they could have raised a kid to be so ungrateful after you knock yourself out to help.

How could Wanda improve the next time? Simple. Walk into the house, graciously greet everyone and turn to her daughter and ask, "What can I do to help you?" Then do it; not what she thinks she should do. Every mother on planet earth with a two and three-year-old would really appreciate help. But she would also appreciate being addressed adult-to-adult and not have her requests ignored or minimized and also experience from her mother a positive attitude of serving as an expression of her love. The positive attitude is the key.

Appropriately Express Your Love Physically

It was our first venture to South America and Venezuela in particular. We emailed our long time missionary friends who had served in Venezuela and asked them to share with us cultural tips. One of the cultural practices is to greet each other with a hug and a light kiss on the cheek.

Quite an entourage greeted the North American team at the airport. Our new Latin friends stuck out their hands to shake ours. We shook their hands, then, gave them a hug and a light kiss on the cheek. We were not prepared for their response. They began to laugh with joy and excitement and were very animated with each other in their conversations while glancing at us. After a period of greeting and waiting for our home assignments, our translator, Bernard Lopez, came up to me and explained, "These people are really surprised at you. They say you are not like other Americans."

I asked why. He responded, "My brother, most Americans who come here to teach just shake hands and stand off but you are very different." What made the difference? We had been coached on what their cultural symbols of love and acceptance were. Whether they were our symbols or whether or not we were comfortable with that form of expressing love and acceptance, it was *their* symbol and custom. But we would have done the same things other Americans have done if we had not been alerted to the local customs.

Appropriate touch can be another vital form of expressing love to your adult child. For some, appropriate hugs are important, for others a handshake can convey it. Others like their hand, arm or shoulder touched. Keith, a friend of mine, likes for his wife to rub his hand, touch his shoulder or rub the back of his neck while he drives. It's not a sexual thing. Those who love to be touched in a non-sexual way really enjoy sitting close to a person while watching a movie. A light kiss on the cheek may be desired by another. But what is important is that the physical expression be totally acceptable to your adult child. Under no circumstances is it to be forced on them. It is their boundary that needs to be respected, not yours. It is appropriate for you to have your own boundaries which they must also respect.

Beware that some adult children do not want you to touch them at all. Of course, that is also their choice, not yours. They may have reasons that have nothing to do with you. One out of every four girls was molested as a child and one out of every six boys have experienced sexual violations, and you may be clueless that it even happened.

Share Your Love Symbols

Healthy relationships are a two-way street. Here we have emphasized our responsibility to learn to express our love and respect from our grown kids' perspective. But the best relationships are a two-way street. It may be awkward at first for you to share with your kids what your symbols of love are, but I strongly suggest you have an informal evening together and allow them to share with you what you can do to make them feel loved. Then, share with them ways you feel loved. Take the bold step to share with your kids how they can best express their love for you and to you like Jesus did. "If you love Me, keep My commandments" (John 14:15).

CHAPTER 7

Points to Ponder

1. Choose to demonstrate love and respect.
2. Adjust your approach to expressing your love.
3. Realize your kids' symbols of love are different than yours.
4. Discover their symbols of love and respect.
5. Verbalize your compliments.
6. Express love through respect.
7. Invest quality time.
8. Share thoughtful gifts where appropriate.
9. Love them both in deed and in truth.
10. Express your love physically.
11. Share your love symbols.

CHAPTER 7

Love and Respect Them

Small Group Questions

1. In what ways did your parents fill or fail to fill your love and respect buckets? How did it influence your life? What have you done to deal with empty childhood buckets in adulthood?

2. How have you had to adjust your approach to expressing your love and respect to your adult children? What did you learn from it that would help other parents?

3. How different are your adult children's love symbols than yours?

4. How did you discover the love and respect symbols of your grown kids and their spouses?

5. What challenges have you experienced giving verbal compliments? How were they received?

6. Why do you think sons and sons-in-law filter any expressions of love through respect? What are some creative ways you have found effective in demonstrating respect?

7. Why is it so hard for parents to spend quality time with their adult children? What changes have you had to make personally to make that happen?

8. What are some creative ways you have been able to share thoughtful gifts? What was their response?

9. What practical acts of service have you found effective with your adult children? What have you learned *not* to do?

10. How have you been able to demonstrate appropriate physical affection if you did not experience it growing up? How was it received when you demonstrated physical affection in an adult-to-adult relationship?

11. How open have your adult children been to discuss what you would want them to do so you feel loved? How did you bring it up? What would you suggest to this group to do or not do when approaching their kids on this subject? What effect did it have on the relationship?

CHAPTER 8

Respect Mutual Boundaries

The call came late one night. Margaret was in tears. She had been a friend of the family for years. The crisis tonight was over her husband Richard's adult daughter from a previous marriage. Her second marriage was breaking up and she was planning to move back home with her dad and Margaret. No discussion, it was a done deal. The daughter announced her plan to return home. Dad said nothing and Margaret was devastated by the intrusion. Margaret just sobbed, "I can't take it again."

Identify the Source of Relational Pain

The main source of pain that parents experience with their grown children boils down to a failure to establish and maintain appropriate *boundaries*. The failure of the parents or young adults to identify the need for boundaries and the failure to establish and maintain them often results in fractured relationships. "Change can only begin when parents understand the healthy boundaries that are necessary to the parent and child relationship."[63] And I would add, maintain those boundaries.

Boundaries are God's Idea

God is the one who established the principle of boundaries, limitations or circles of responsibility. The first parents were given free reign of the entire Garden of Eden to enjoy. God established one boundary or limitation with His adult children. "And the Lord God commanded the man, saying, 'Of every tree of the garden you may freely eat; but of the tree of the Knowledge of Good and Evil, you shall not eat.'" Then God established the consequences if they did violate that boundary, "For in the day that you eat of it you shall surely die" (Gen 2:16, 17). Adam and Eve chose to violate God's only boundary by eating the forbidden fruit. God called that a transgression. The word transgression is made up of two words, "trans" which means "across" and "gression" which means "to walk". Together it means to walk across a boundary or established limitation.

God established a boundary the Old Testament for those who were not priests. King Uzziah, out of pride, chose to go into the temple where only a priest was to enter. Uzziah then offered incense that was only to be offered by a priest. God judged him with leprosy (2 Chron. 26:16-20).

Boundaries are essential in establishing and maintaining healthy relationships. Cloud and Townsend describe them as tools that define what is me and what is not me, what is mine and what is not mine. Boundaries show me where I end and someone else begins. They lead us to a sense of ownership of our space and I would add, our responsibility.[64]

Boundaries define what we are to own and take responsibility for or what we are *not* to take responsibility for. Failure to take responsibility for your own life distorts your choices and options. "People with boundary problems usually have distorted attitudes about responsibility."[65]

Margaret's emotional pain was justified. Her husband saw no need to establish any boundaries with his grown daughter, let alone attempt to maintain any. Because boundaries were a foreign concept to his daughter, too, she felt entitled to just move back home without permission or consulting the parents. Therefore, she did not take any responsibility for her past choices or the consequences of her choices. This distorted her attitudes and heightened her sense of entitlement, "What's yours is mine and what's mine is mine." Because Richard was clueless about biblical limitations, he felt obligated to take back his daughter and expected Margaret, his wife, to emotionally and financially support the return of this "frequent flyer" who was returning home for the second time.

No Boundaries, No Peace

Boundary-setting can be especially difficult in relationships between parents and their adult children. People who were raised in families with enmeshed or blurred boundaries often have difficulty identifying the need for creating healthy boundaries now in their adult relationships.[66]

Because boundaries help establish who we are, loose boundaries mix up the identities of the parents and the adult children which results in creating an enmeshed family system. They cannot separate their own needs and responsibilities from each other, resulting in their own feelings and identities becoming submerged. As a result, they become over- dependent on each other and cannot make healthy adult choices because their identities and responsibilities are blurred. Whether it is the parent or the adult child, the one with the blurred or weak boundaries will always let anyone do to them whatever they wish. And the result? They can never say, "No" like God said to Adam and Eve.[67] Richard could not say, "No" to his adult daughter, even though it deeply wounded his wife.

Why can't we say, "No"? Submerged under all the complicated details of the parent-child relationship is a deep-seated fear that we will be rejected and abandoned if we say, "No." This fear of abandonment is the primary dynamic beneath most dependent and addictive behaviors.[68] This fear can be as strong in Christians as non-believers, even though the believer knows intellectually that God will never leave him (Hebrews 13:5). However, this fear of abandonment may have more power in his mind than biblical truth.

What do boundaries that are too rigid look like? Neither the parent nor child is allowed to enter each other's world of feeling. Needs and identities are kept secret and separate. The adult child feels isolated and aloof. They just can't connect with anyone. If they leave the home that confuses independence with isolation. Any kind of feeling gets translated as weakness and dependence. Thus, they are afraid to express their feelings.

Rigid parents never play, rarely empathize, don't reflect care and seem distant and detached. The whole family seems cold and empty. As a result, children with dysfunctional family boundaries stand an immense risk of developing severe emotional problems, compulsions and addictions as they grow up.[69] No boundaries, no peace.

Recognize What Healthy Boundaries Are

What would healthy parent-adult child boundaries look like? First, you are able to let people get as close or stay as distant as you choose. You can make the close-distant shift according to what is appropriate at any given time without a negative reaction. Therefore, you are able to let people come and go without feeling fearful, guilty or experiencing loss. As a result, you can allow people to check in and communicate with each other because they want to, not because they have to out of obligation.

When it comes to activities, you can choose to participate in them jointly or separately or not at all. You are able to do this because your relationships are strong but not confining, controlling or exclusive. You can participate out of choice, not obligation. You are free to be led by God's Spirit and not the fear of others' conditional acceptance, rejection or disapproval (Romans 8:14). The family roles and responsibilities can be negotiated with each other respectfully when conflict arises. This can be done on an adult-to-adult basis with mutual respect.[70]

The common thread that is woven all through these characteristics is that each person is viewed and respected as an adult and no one is making another person dependent on them to act as their security blanket in life. I personally believe that the co-dependent person has made another person act in the place of God on their behalf. They become their idol. No one with a bedrock security in their personal relationship with Christ will make another human their ultimate security in this life.

The Apostle Paul said that for him to live is Christ (no one else) and if he should die, it would be gain, not loss (Phil. 1:21). Christ, not people, was his foundation for life. True, he knew human abandonment. He confided in Timothy in one of his last letters while in prison, "At my first defense no one stood with me, but all forsook me ... But the Lord stood with me and strengthened me ..." (2 Tim. 4:16,17). It was clear that God, not people, was his ultimate source of security. What is your ultimate source of security?

Establish Boundaries with Your Married Children

At our oldest daughter's wedding when I said, "Today ends a relationship we've had for 21 years", I had the classic "leave and cleave" verse in Genesis 2:24 in mind. "Therefore a man shall leave his father and mother and be joined to his wife, and they shall become one flesh." I have heard some mothers of daughters say, "But that says 'a man' not a woman." On the contrary, in Eph. 5:22-24, it is clear she is to be subject to her husband, not her mother or her mother-in-law. I went on to say that today begins a new relationship that her mother and I look forward to based on a new set of boundaries. No, these were not easy to establish and maintain, but they had to be established.

DeeDee and Roger lived next door to us for seven years in the duplex we owned. Whenever we went next door for any reason, we always knocked on the door. Why? Boundaries respect privacy. I will confess the grandchildren did not knock on our door. They frequently came over to our side in their pajamas to have breakfast. They insisted our cereal and milk always tasted better than theirs.

Right from the beginning we talked adult-to-adult with Roger and DeeDee. We did not pry into their personal relationship or financial business or evaluate how they spent their money. They were free to tell us what they wanted us to know.

How your adult children keep or fail to keep their house or apartment is completely their responsibility. If you barge in and start criticizing the condition of their home or apartment, you, not they, have violated a boundary. You can mention you have a little extra time and ask if there is anything you can do to help them. Asking permission is called respect.

We have devoted a whole chapter to grandparenting and grandchildren. But one simple boundary here to keep in mind is that grandchildren are *not* your children. You are *not* the parents and they are *not* your responsibility. The only exception would be in cases of abuse.

This boundary is tough to respect. Grandchildren, not our birth children, are our glory and joy (Proverbs 17:6). It can tear us up inside emotionally to see them go through negative circumstances and we feel completely helpless.

Boundaries regarding our married kids are easier to identify. but what if they are single and are still at home or single and living on their own? What do appropriate limits look like now?

Boundaries and Single Adults

There is usually something inside of us that prevents us from viewing our non-married, adult children as self-contained, responsible adults. This is especially true if they are single and have not left home or are single and have returned home.

Returning to the Nest

Why do over 55% of young adults between the ages of eighteen and twenty-five still live at home or have returned home? The most common reason adult children return home is related to a lack of maturity.[71] Just because they possess an adult body and have a college education does not mean they have grown up emotionally. They may still possess a core belief that they are entitled to be taken care of like they have been all their life. Richard's daughter held this belief. She viewed her first two marriages as "trial marriages." Some have referred to first marriages as "starter marriages" hoping the second or third marriage would be a winner, although most research indicates the divorce rate is higher. Although they are adults, they have failed to put away the childish thinking of dependence and assume the adult role of independence (I Cor. 13:11).

Surprisingly, many did not want to leave home in the first place. Why? They preferred to stay at home to enjoy a more affluent lifestyle for as long as possible. Studies repeatedly indicate that young adults from more affluent families are the most likely to remain at home.[72] Some also return home because they have been so scarred from failed attempts to make it in the adult world and they return battle weary and worse for the wear. Often the problems were there before they left and now they need to be faced. One of the boundaries parents must establish *before* they return home is that they get appropriate help to address their fears, insecurities and complete any unfinished business in the task of growing up.

Agree Upon the Purpose for Their Return

It cannot be stated strongly enough the importance of determining *before* they return what their purpose for returning is. Are they coming home to re-group and to devise a game plan to return to independence or to return home "for awhile" because they are tired of battling life and want to hide in the security of their parents' home?[73] The former are referred to as *planners*, the latter are called *strugglers*. Others have referred to them as "boomerang kids" – an adult who moved out of his parents' house but later returned.

Approximately one out of ten U.S. adults, ages 25-34, are now living with their parents according to the National Survey of Families and Households. This is confirmed by the U.S. Census Bureau. Sons are nearly twice as likely as daughters to return home. The average stay is six months to two years.

Often the reaction to the boomerang kid depends on where you are in life. If you are retired or about to retire, your resentment may be understandable. You may have to put your retirement on hold until your child gets his life in order. Yet, if you are already retired you may also be wondering how they are going to support you if you need it in your old age. It is rarely an ideal situation.

Michael floundered a lot in life after high school. Life was a party. He lived away from home and supported his self-gratifying lifestyle. A series of events brought him to a place of turning his life around and he started to make something of himself. He asked his parents, who had been enjoying their empty nest, if he could move back home with the agreement he would return to the University, get acceptable grades and earn his own spending money. Michael was a planner. I recently learned that he graduated with honors and is now in a masters' program and being considered for a good job in his field. He and his parents had a plan and made the plan work. His parents helped with the education. Both kept their commitment.

Planners who already have their trade or education save money for a specific goal which ultimately gives them the independence they desire. They are also aware that they are temporarily a burden to their parents. They are willing to contribute financially to the home and will still get some type of job while looking for a job in their career field. Planners are not sponges.

Establish Financial Responsibility

Your son or daughter may have returned to live with you because they could not manage their own money. Allowing them to stay with you and permitting them to do what they have always done but expecting different results is the definition of insanity. Your first step is to have them establish some financial responsibility by contributing to the household expenses whether it is needed or not. Agreements about what you can expect from them financially and they from you should be determined early and modified as situations change for either of you.

It is a fact of life that it costs money to live on their own so they need to feel the pressure of that responsibility at home. You can either collect a regular contribution toward the household expenses or save it and give it back later as a nest egg to help them get started.

If they are not able to contribute financially immediately, then negotiate some home responsibilities or repairs. One of our staff members' sons moved back home because of some self-destructive habits that needed to be corrected. Meanwhile, he did a lot of repairs around the house that had been delayed because of other family priorities. While he was working at home, he was also working at getting his driver's license back and diligently seeking employment. It is not a matter of either/or, it is a matter of both.

You must be fully convinced yourself that they can make it on their own and that they need to take steps to get the training and experience that will allow them to succeed. If you want them to become self-sufficient adults, you must treat them as such and not as an incompetent child. When you are convinced yourself that they cannot make it on their own, you will find it hard to say "No" to their unreasonable requests. The most boundary-setting word is "No".[74] It is usually parental guilt and fear that makes parents say "yes" when they should say "no". Saying "yes" is not the morally required answer to every demand although some adult children may believe otherwise.[75]

You may experience some verbal abuse from your adult child in an attempt to put you in your place, that is, to be submissive to his/her will and requests. This may be designed to put you on a guilt trip but usually that guilt is false guilt. God does not lead you by guilt. He leads by His Spirit (Rom. 8:14). Your responsibility is to say what you mean, mean what you say and make absolutely certain your actions and decisions say the same thing your words do.[76] Financial accountability and responsibility are a mark of maturity. If he's unable to provide for his own family and even his parents in dire need, God believes it is an indication he has abandoned the principles of his faith and is viewed to be worse than one who never claimed to be a Christian (I Tim. 5:8).

Parents are Entitled to Know the Finances

If the purpose of the planner's return to the family nest is to save money and to restore their independence, then the parents have a right to be involved in their budgeting process and their financial books should be open. Why? Because the parents are subsidizing the "nester" by providing a home. Nesters often feel entitled to spend their money as they see fit at their parents' expense. Unfortunately, nesters tend to blow their money and have little or nothing to show for it and the subsidizing parents are clueless where their kid stands financially.

Many nesters have a core belief that they are entitled to a rent free, food-free program. Their logic is that the parents will pay and the kid can play. If that is happening in your home, the adult child is not the problem! The parent has failed to establish firm boundaries with the nester.

When you apply for a bank loan, you are required to give a lot of personal information. Why? It is their money they are loaning to you; therefore, they have a right to know how the money is to be used. Your nester is borrowing or using your money (food, rent, utilities), therefore, you have a responsibility to know how he is spending his money. He may balk and try to put you on a guilt trip that you have more money than he does and you need to give it to him without conditions. Suggest he try that logic on a bank.

For the nester, financial accountability may mean that he devises a budget to gain financial independence. Usually if *they* come up with a budget, they are more likely to fulfill it; however it still needs to be agreed upon by all concerned. Remember, one of the reasons the nester returned home was because he could not handle finances appropriately. Part of becoming an adult involves the transition between dependent and independent thinking and living.[77] If your adult child does not have any financial or housekeeping responsibilities in the home, he is still in the role of a dependent child.

Should the adult child not be comfortable in designing a budget with you or on his own, he can go to a financial counselor or church member who is skilled in financial planning. He, then, shares his game plan with you. It is important for nesters and parents to work together to determine their shared goals and expectations on how economic independence is going to be achieved. It would not hurt to have him email you a monthly progress report even if you are in the next room. This prevents you from becoming an "expenditure cop" that grills him on every purchase he makes.

Part of that budget needs to include contributions to the household expenses, payment on student loans and a strategy for saving for the future. If you are not comfortable in having him contribute to the financial responsibilities of the home, then be sure that he is putting into savings what he would normally pay if he was on his own, so that he can feel the pressure of normal expenses that are part of being a responsible adult. It costs to live. It was the God of mercy who established the no-work-no-eat principle (2 Thessalonians 3:10). Pain usually comes before change.

Planners develop a strategy to leave, but strugglers return home to hide and to be taken care of and demonstrate little or no responsibility. Strugglers habitually put off any steps of action to return to independence, make little effort to grow up and definitely take little or no initiative to change.

What does a parent usually do with a struggler? They enable the immature adult to continue to be irresponsible out of fear of being rejected by him. Here is where false guilt creeps into the parents' thinking. They think they are acting in an unloving way to insist their grown child takes responsibility for his life. *Love gives a child what he needs, not what he wants.* Having no plan for independence is a plan for further conflict.

Who Decides Who Comes Home?

It must be very clear that it is the parents' decision, not the child's, if the adult child is to move back home. Why? God has given the parents the responsibility for their home and it is their decision who stays or does not stay. Here is where Margaret was deeply hurt. Richard made the decision to allow his daughter to return home. The daughter announced her arrival and dad caved in. In his mind, he and his daughter were a family before there was a Margaret. Dad, not the daughter, is the one who failed to be responsible here. In dysfunctional relationships there are few, if any, established and maintained boundaries.

No adult child has the right to force himself on another adult. Grown kids and parents are to relate adult-to-adult, even if one of them is not acting like an adult. It is not a child who is returning home, it is an adult, even if he is not acting like an adult. God still views him as an adult whether the parents do or not. Failure to understand that the grown child is an adult is a perfect set up for further conflict and for bad decision making on the part of the parents.

It is just as dysfunctional for the single adult to revert back to being a dependent teen as it is for a parent to revert back to the role of parenting a dependent teen. You do not parent adult children. Why? That keeps them in a mental state of childhood and they never grow up emotionally.

It must go without saying that all the rules, roles, guidelines, boundaries, responsibilities and expectations need to be clarified before they move in.[78] Usually emergency circumstances cause the adult children to abruptly return. Even so, every day that passes that this task has not been undertaken only makes the process more difficult later.

If they are allowed to return home, the parents have a responsibility to relate to their adult child as an adult with respect. The knife cuts both ways. The adult child has the responsibility to treat his parents with honor and respect also.

Maintain Your Family Values

Parents are to maintain the family values in their home even though they may differ from those of their adult children. You have every right and responsibility before God to maintain the godly home you have established (Joshua 24:15). If the grown children plan to continue to live at home, parents have a right to ask them to respect the values of the parents just as if they were living in someone else's home.[79]

Don't fall into the trap of thinking you're forcing your values on them. It is a matter of them showing deference to and respect for your values while they are living in your home. They are in your space; not vice versa. They are not being forced to live at home. It is a mutual choice, and if they choose to live with you, they are also choosing to respect your values.

Distinguish Between Moral and Management Issues

House rules or management issues need to be brought out into the open immediately so that everyone's expectations are stated and clarified. Are they going to be a big part of the house rituals like sitting down for dinner together or are they going to come and go at will? Establish what both you and they can live with. Do not expect them to call this family council together to decide on these issues. You will have to initiate this discussion.

When Gary and Sylvia's adult daughter lived at home, the daughter's household habits made it difficult for them to get a good night's sleep. She would come in at all hours of the night, fix herself a snack and turn on the TV which kept her parents awake.

It was suggested to Gary and Sylvia that rather than just lay down a rule of no TV past 11:00 pm, they clearly state that mom and dad need their sleep because they both leave early for work. For house management purposes, there has to be a limit on the TV use. As an adult she can stay out as late as she wants, but because it disrupts the family's ability to function well, it is not a moral issue; it is a home management issue.

Should the daughter be out all hours of the night? That is her responsibility and choice. But if it prevents the parents from fulfilling their work responsibilities, it now becomes a management issue. Home management includes respect for privacy (theirs and yours), the use of the phone, computer, possessions and respect for the family schedule.

Some parents can't sleep if their adult children are not home and safe. The sleep issue is the parents' problem, not the adult child's problem. As a parent you may have an unhealthy need to control your adult child. You need to explore the fear behind your control issue. Even if he is quiet and not disruptive and comes and goes as he pleases, if that freedom bothers you, you need to have an adult-to-adult talk. You should inform him that you cannot sleep, you worry about his safety and for those reasons he has one of two choices. One, respect your house routine and come home at a reasonable time or, two, make other living arrangements. It is not a moral issue; it is a management issue. You have the ultimate responsibility for your home; therefore, you have the ultimate authority for the home, *not* the adult child.

If they want to smoke and you prefer they not smoke inside, kindly ask them to smoke outside for your own health reasons, not necessarily moral reasons. If you prefer them not to drink alcohol in your home, then it must be made clear that it is not to be brought into the house. It is also fair to inform them that if you notice they are drunk and are driving a vehicle, you will report them to the police as you would any drunk driver or the police may have to inform you that your adult son just killed a young mother while driving drunk. It's your choice.

If they want to bring a boyfriend or girlfriend over and "sleep" together, you have a right to inform (or remind) them this arrangement is not acceptable to you. This is a moral issue. You are not going to prevent their immoral behavior with this request but you are responsible not to allow it in your home. If they leave, you did not kick them out. They had to leave because of their choice not to respect your values. We have to remind ourselves that our adult children are sexually immoral because they live in a very sexually permissive society. Immorality is glamorized by their friends, TV, movies and the Internet, plus, most of them have a fear of commitment because of their dual fears of divorce and abandonment.[80]

Avoid two extremes, denial and dogged condemnation by making each contact with them an occasion to condemn and to lecture their immoral behavior. This could drive them deeper into the immoral commitment just to spite you and could damage any future relationship with them should they marry.

If the adult child is presently exploiting your home, he may not be the problem. You may be. You have the responsibility to confront the issue(s) and renegotiate an acceptable arrangement and take responsible steps to correct it. If you are unable to confront an irresponsible adult child living in your home, you have the problem and should seek professional counsel to deal with your own feelings.

This is not a tough love issue; it is a responsible love issue. You must give them what they need, not what they want.

Avoidance only buries the problem, later to resurface again and again unresolved. Yes, it is still in your circle of responsibility to grant them the same common courtesies you would grant to anyone else while they are going through these growing experiences.[81]

Distinguish Between Acceptance and Approval

Acceptance means you are just acknowledging what is a reality. The kids may be engaging in an immoral relationship. You have to step out of this "safe" place of denial into the painful realm of reality. Approval means you affirm something as good or right.[82] You cannot affirm from your biblical perspective that their sexual relationship is good; rather, it is totally wrong (Eph. 5:3). But showing love and respect is not approval of sin. Even God does not stop loving us as believers when we sin. He grieves over our sin (Eph. 4:30). Nor does God remove His grace (favor) from us when we sin because it is a free gift, not an earned right (Eph. 2:8-9).

How can you relate to an adult child who is making poor moral choices? Choose to relate to them as persons who are still created in the image of God (Gen. 1:26). Listen, consider their points and affirm their logic and perspective when possible (James 1:19). In honesty, disagree where you must. Ask probing questions without sounding like a prosecuting attorney. Use a pleasant tone of voice, shake their hand and give an occasional hug. You can appreciate the person while not approving of their behavior. Do their bad moral choices hurt? Yes! Do they hurt God? Yes! (Eph. 4:30). Share your own hurts as a result of their wrong moral choices but avoid using your pain as a means to manipulate change.[83]

You may have to remind yourself that your adult child still loves you and may need you. He knows down deep exactly how you are hurt by his behavior. He knows that your continued love does not mean that you approve of what he is doing or that you are going to violate your own values.[84] It is God's responsibility to convict him of sin, not yours (John 16:8). Let him know why you think his choices are unhealthy and wrong, but balance that with the reassurance of your continued love and prayers. After you have clearly stated your position back off and continue to demonstrate your sincere love for him.

What if They are Gay?

Few things devastate parents more than to have their adult child admit he/she is a homosexual or a lesbian.

How does the concept of boundaries apply if they insist that their homosexual or lesbian partner comes to your home for a visit and to spend the night? As hard as it may sound, this would be an opportunity for you to demonstrate consistency in your convictions. Apply the same principle to your adult child's "partner" that you would apply to the unmarried opposite-sex friend.

It is crucial here that you don't display a double standard to an opposite-sex sin and a same-sex sin. They are both displeasing to God and damaging to each other (Rom. 1:18-32). You would request any unmarried or heterosexual couple to sleep in separate rooms. Simply apply the same standard based on your convictions in both instances. If they choose not to stay in your home because of your standards, that is their choice. You have to respect their choice to leave in the same way you expect them to honor your standards if they stayed. You did not "kick them out", their choice made them leave.

Diligently work to build the relationship on every piece of common ground you can. The only chance you have for any possible influence in your children's lives is through the relationship that already exists between you and them.[85] If there's no relationship, then there is little or no influence.

It's Time to Say "Goodbye!"

Most returnees prevail on us as parents in a crisis or looming crisis. Ideally, you should mutually agree on a reasonable time limit for their stay before they move back in. Circumstances may necessitate a brief calming down of stressful emotions before they are ready for rational dialog about their future plans.

But it is important to set some goals and a target date for their departure which will serve both as motivation for movement and direction. You cannot force them to grow up, but you can help your child by not always creating the safe harbor that prevents that growth from happening.[86] Pain almost always precedes growth (James 1:2-4).

It may be that your child needs an anchor for his soul spiritually and emotionally more than a safe harbor in which to hide from himself. There is a difference between temporary repairs and indefinite residency. It may be time for him to establish his relationship with God and allow Him to be his anchor (Heb. 6:19). If you relieve the pain, you reduce the need for him to grow up.

Yes, time limits may need to be renegotiated as long as the goal remains to develop both spiritual and emotional maturity and independence. This may call for some time and expense invested into professional counseling to help them deal with their fears and anxieties that keep them stuck in their parents' harbor.

When it's time to go, avoid stating, "The door is always open." They are always welcome to visit. "Frequent flyers" that keep falling back into the nest need to know it is disappointing both to you and to them because of the stress it creates.

Respect Their Religious Preferences

Most parents have had the same struggles that God has had with His children. The prophet Isaiah spoke for God when he said, "I have nourished and brought up children, and they have rebelled against me" (Isaiah 1:2b). What do you do if your kids choose a different belief system than yours?

First, it is in your circle of responsibility to respect your adult children's religious preferences whether you agree with them or not. Acknowledgment does not mean agreement. You have to acknowledge the reality that it is what it is. Yes, it hurts when they choose a different belief system than yours. Because religious beliefs are often tied strongly to our emotions, when they make religious choices that differ from ours, we can feel a great deal of pain like God does.[87]

You are now faced with two choices. First, you can abandon them, write them off or reject them because you disagree with their choice. You can be harsh, condemning, rigid, angry and explosive, but these responses are guaranteed to lose any opportunity to influence their thinking in the future and forfeit the possibility of any relationship.[88]

The second choice you have is to continue to relate to them in a respectful way and keep communication open. Work at making contacts with them pleasant experiences as much as you are able to (Rom 12:18). You may even visit their religious sessions, if appropriate. Research their religion. Exchange ideas in an honest, non-condemning way. One advantage you have is that biblical Christianity can always stand investigation, but cults or other religions cannot. Always remain calm because this is one issue that is not going to be changed by your might or your power. It will be done by God's Spirit (Zech. 4:6).

The more authentically you practice what you preach, the more respect they may have for you and your beliefs. The opposite is also true. When that has been the case, you may need to ask for forgiveness for not being an example to them. It is all right to acknowledge how you have failed them in that regard in the past. You might discover that your honesty and vulnerability may just open some significant closed doors.

A reality you may have to face is that you cannot change or control them. You are limited to being an influence. You also have the power of prayer and praying friends that may open the door of their hearts that has previously been chained shut. This is especially true when they see you acknowledge the reality that religions and spiritual beliefs and practices are ultimately in their circle of responsibility as adults.

We've All Worked Hard

Bob and Sue have worked hard all their lives. He has held several key positions in industry and was able to retire before the magical age of 65. Sue taught kindergarten and grades 1

- 3 for 28 years. Her school honored her with an outstanding retirement party. That's the good news.

The sad news is that their son and two daughters still struggle in many areas of responsibility even though their parents provided college education for all of them. Bob and Sue are not rich, but their basic needs are met. With the huge needs their adult children present to them regularly, they have one big question, "How do we dispense our resources wisely? How do we be good stewards with what God has entrusted to us?" That's the next issue we must address in chapter nine.

CHAPTER 8

Points to Ponder

1. Identify the source of relational pain.
2. Understand the value of appropriate boundaries.
3. Recognize what healthy boundaries are.
4. Establish boundaries with your married children.
5. Agree upon the purpose for the return of an adult child to your home.
6. Know your child's finances if he is returning because of financial problems.
7. Understand you have the last word regarding who can return home.
8. Maintain your family values.
9. Distinguish between moral and management issues.
10. Distinguish between acceptance and approval.
11. Be consistent with your gay children.
12. Identify the time to say "goodbye."
13. Establish financial responsibility.
14. Respect their religious preferences.

CHAPTER 8

Respect Mutual Boundaries

Small Group Questions

1. How did you first come to understand the concept of boundaries? Describe what you believe boundaries are.

2. Share some of the difficulties you have had with your grown children related to boundary issues.

3. How have you had to establish boundaries with your adult children? What was their response?

4. What boundary challenges did you face when your grown child returned home? How did you deal with them and what was your child's response?

5. Describe what financial arrangements you made either with the grown child still living at home or after he moved out and later returned? How were these arrangements worked out? What adjustments did you have to make?

6. In what ways have your grown children challenged your personal values?

7. What are some basic management type issues that you had to address either when your grown child returned home or remained in your home?

8. What are some moral issues you have had to address? How did you approach them? What was your child's response? What would you do differently?

9. What has been your experience in making a distinction between accepting (acknowledging) a questionable issue and approving (disapproving) a questionable issue? How did you do it? What was your child's response? Describe what you had to go through to make that distinction.

10. What experience have you had working with your adult child to work on his financial issues if he either has never left or has returned to live in your home? What did you learn from that experience that would be helpful to share with other parents?

11. In what ways have your adult children challenged your belief system? How did you respond? What scripture became more meaningful to you through those experiences? What advice would you give to parents who are going through that experience now?

CHAPTER 9

Dispense Resources Wisely

The wedding was beautiful. Michelle and Greg were off on their honeymoon to Florida. The pictures they emailed back to us were terrific. Later in the week they even called us on our cell phone to say, "Hello."

We have had a family cell phone plan since Michelle went away to college. Even though she was scarcely working part time she said, "I want to help pay for my share of the phone." And she did. Because the cell phone company family plan works while she is married, she still pays her share of the bill. Why? She feels responsible for herself as an adult. The word "entitlement" has never come up. She never tried to manipulate us to pay the whole bill by saying, "You can afford it." Unfortunately, that is not the thinking of many adult children today. Many believe you owe them your resources now! What are the principles you need to consider before you dispense your resources, *especially* to your adult children?

Resist the Entitlement Trap

The English word "entitle" comes from a Latin word, *"intitulus"* which literally means to bestow a name or a special title or position on a person. After that person is given this special title, he now claims all the rights and privileges that come with that title. Others are now obligated to give him all that his position entitled him to have. Unfortunately, many adult children either bestow upon themselves that special title (position) or believe their family association as son or daughter entitles them to rights and privileges that were never envisioned by their parents. This logic gives them the license to exploit their parents' resources. For them this license does not expire.[89]

Many grown children believe their self-bestowed title or birth family title should grant them peace, prosperity and an equal lifestyle of their parents. They seriously believe, "What's mine is mine and what's yours is mine." As a result they believe they have the bestowed right to take your stuff without asking and violate your privacy at will. They rationalize that what they take, you didn't need or they believe you can afford to give it up. Their reasoning may go deeper, believing you owe it to them because that is what parents are for. This reasoning takes away the parents' right and responsibility to say, "No" – the most important boundary word in any language.

They are acting out the core beliefs of their heart (Prov. 23:7) believes they have a special title or position and they are free either to demand what they want or to take what they want. You cannot stop that thinking but you must not allow yourself to believe it and think you are trapped with no options. The three characteristics of adulthood are choice, responsibility and consequences. You do have choices even though the consequences of those choices may result in an angry response, manipulation, threats, rejection and future disconnecting and withholding visitation of your grandkids.

In contrast, God, by His grace, grants you a position as His son or daughter. All the benefits that come to you from that grace-based position are given not because of any merit of your own. They are not entitled privileges that you can demand (Eph. 2:8,9; 1:6,7).

It is almost useless to argue with an entitled-based offspring. You can acknowledge their position, then, clearly state you have a different position. Tell them you will think about their request and get back to them. This allows you time to separate logic from emotion. It will also give you time to prepare an answer, knowing full well it may not be accepted unless it is in their favor. Do not, under any circumstances, reinforce the entitlement lie by caving in to their perceived right to exploit you. If you do, the hand that took it from you will return again and again.

Distinguish Between Affordability and Responsibility

One of the guilt trip tactics your grown kids may attempt to manipulate you with is the statement, "You can afford it." If you bite on this bait you will get hooked into a dead end argument. The issue is *not* affordability; it is responsibility. There are six questions each parent must ask themselves before they respond to a request.

- Do I have *time* to fulfill this request?
- Do I have the *skill* or knowledge to fulfill this request?
- Do I have the *power* of authority to undertake this request?
- Do I have the *energy* to do this?
- Do I have the *resources* to comply with this request?
- Do I have the *responsibility* to fulfill this request?

Any of these can be factors in your life that could prevent you from granting the request. Yet, the key question in dispensing your resources wisely is to first come to terms with the responsibility issue. Entitled kids will insist it is your responsibility. You have to take a step back and ask God if it is indeed your responsibility or are you being manipulated.

You are a steward of all your resources physically, mentally, emotionally and financially and you are responsible directly to God, not the kids. There will be a special day when we, as believers, will have to appear before the Judgment seat of Christ for the purpose of being rewarded for our deeds, whether good or bad (2 Cor. 5:10). If they are good, we will be rewarded greatly for them. If they are bad, we will experience loss of rewards, not salvation. The salvation issue is settled already for the believer. As stewards, you are to be responsible and faithful for the stewardship of your resources. In fact, you are required by God to be found trustworthy because of *how* you dispense your resources. Trust is earned, not demanded and you earn trust by wise stewardship (I Cor. 4:2).

If your adult children are asking you for help to pay their electric bill after they just brought home a new high definition flat screen TV, you may have to remind yourself that their unwise use of their resources does not obligate you to compensate for their irresponsibility. A high definition flat screen sold on the secondary market could pay for a lot of electricity. But chances are they borrowed the money or used a credit card to purchase it and, therefore, they may not be able to sell it. At this point they need professional financial counsel, not a bail out. Whatever you do, do not volunteer to be their financial advisor. Rarely does that work. It is not wise to assume that role because of emotional entanglement. That is the very reason most surgeons do not operate on members of their own family even though they have the skill to do it.

Once you establish in your own mind that you are not your grown kids' walking ATM machine, you are free to refer them to those who are skilled in helping indebted people to reach financial freedom. Constantly remind yourself that God, not you, has promised to supply their needs from His unlimited resources, not yours (Phil. 4:19). Financial pressure may drive them to God, but if you relieve the pressure, they will habitually turn to you, rather than to God and even a qualified financial counselor.

A bond may always remain between you and your kids, but that bond does not obligate you to support them financially for life. The reverse is also true. Your kids are not bound to bail you out over and over because of your irresponsible decisions. Often kids do not contact you unless they want something from you. This is a mutual dysfunction that needs to be corrected by applying the biblical principles of personal responsibility. It is part of God's plan to allow our adult children to experience need in order to accomplish two things; first, learn how to be content with food and clothes (I Tim. 6:8) and second, to learn how to cry out to God for divine provision (Luke 11:9-13).

The apostle Paul did not learn how to be content by simply reading a parchment manuscript. He experienced both abundance and need and explained to the Philippian believers the secret of his contentment (Phil. 4:11-12). It was his relationship with Christ and not the presence or absence of material things. He learned through personal experience! If we fail to let our kids learn these lessons, they will return to the role of entitled persons and demand it from you. A smart man learns from his mistakes, but a wise man learns from the mistakes of others. They can learn from wise counsel, but sooner or later that wise counsel will get tested in real life. It is God's goal for your kids to know from personal experience that they can do anything God wants them to do through Christ who gives them the strength (Phil. 4:13).

Stop All Enabling Practices

Most adult children want to be independent on their own, but some of them may not act like that is their goal. A grown child's fear may keep him depending on you to do for him what he is fully capable of doing for himself. That is the heart of enabling. He is depending on you to provide the means, opportunity, power or authority to make something happen that he is able to do for himself.

Enabling your child to be irresponsible can be compared to breaking the legs of a healthy child so you can carry him the rest of his life. No healthy adult would do that, but if you choose to finance your adult child's road to perpetual failure and irresponsibility, you are crippling him for life while preventing him from achieving independence. An adult who fails to stand on his own two feet financially is still a child in an adult body. As an adult you must learn to live within your means and learn from your failures, especially where spending is concerned.[90] Managing a paycheck by paying obligations first and buying discretionary items second is a strong indication of financial responsibility. Making these kinds of decisions and accepting consequences demonstrates a great deal of emotional responsibility.[91]

When you continue to make it possible for your kids to be irresponsible, it is *never* for their benefit. Sadly, it is for *your* benefit. Yes, yours! Why? The truth of the matter is that there are at least four reasons we do not even want to look at what we are doing.

First, there may be a fact that you, as parents, do not want to face. You may not want to acknowledge the reality of your kids' immaturity or failure because that may reflect back on your parenting.

Second, there may be emotions you do not want to feel. You may not want to feel the guilt that may be there or the shame behind it. You may not want to have feelings of disappointment or failure. Fear of the future as to relationships or financial security could be controlling you now. Many countries have the cultural pattern of letting their kids have their way or even treating them like kings in hopes that they will take care of them in their old age.

Third, there may be a responsibility you do not want to assume. You may have to ask forgiveness from your kids for spoiling them or failing to train them to be financially responsible, hoping they would learn later. You may have to do the responsible thing and say, "No" when you know that is not going to be received well. You have to take responsibility for your own emotions and deal with them in a biblical way.

Finally, there may be motives you don't want to admit. One such motive is selfishness. Enabling irresponsibility is not done for the benefit of your adult children; it is primarily for *your* benefit. You don't want them to feel pain because you will feel that pain and you don't want to feel it. So, you selfishly do an irresponsible thing to protect yourself. Here is where some professional counseling could be of benefit. There might be some pain from your own childhood that prevents you from stopping the enabling of your children.

Encourage Them to Fish

A wise old man once said, "Give a man a fish and he will eat for a day. Teach him to fish and he will eat for a lifetime." This was one of the primary goals you have as parents. It is your desire for your kids to leave home, to make a living and manage their resources well. For most of us that happened, but for some, we are still providing the fish. If you are still in the fish supplying business for your adult child, your first step is to confess your part in that failure to teach him to fish. That is hard. Most of us have had to ask our kids' forgiveness for some part of our parenting. Why? None of us are perfect parents.

Many well-educated kids know how to fish, but they are choosing not to even cast their lines. Why? They see no benefit in being self-sufficient, especially when their parents protect them from experiencing financial pain. Pain is a motivator. It is a gift from God. It is a notifier of a need that should be addressed. Otherwise we could experience a premature death. Financial pain and stress can notify your kids of a need to put away their childish ways of spending and grow up to be financially responsible (I Cor. 13:11).

What if you have been an enabler and a fish supplier to your able-bodied grown kids? After you have confessed your failure and asked for forgiveness, it's now time to take the next step. Stop compensating them for their choice to not be self-sufficient. You might discover that their pain of financial withdrawal might result in gaining the desire to get a life supporting job.

Gradually Reduce the Flow

Space will not allow a what-to-do list that fits every situation, however the principle of gradual reduction seems to work in most cases. If you have a child who has never left home, go shopping for an apartment with them and select one with them. Then, offer to pay the first month's rent and reduce it monthly in amounts that have been agreed upon at the beginning. The same approach goes for car payments, car and medical insurance. Basically, no one pays any of these things for us as adults.

God may be harder on your adult child than you are, but He is full of grace and mercy. Recall the no-work-no-eat passage in 2 Thess. 3:10. New Testament scholar, Dr. Thomas L. Constable's comments are very telling here when he states, "The individuals in view were not those who could not work. They were not to be supported by other Christians out of a sense of charity. The loving thing to do for those drones was to let them go hungry so they would be forced to do right and go to work. No Christian who is able, but unwilling, to work should be maintained by others who labor on his behalf."[92]

These are the operational principles in God's family. Are they the same in your family? If your grown kids are eating your food, using your utilities, car, home, computers, credit cards and are spacing out on computer games all night and sleeping half the day, they do not have a problem, you do!

You have given them the title of king or queen and they are now collecting their entitlements that go with the position.

Test Your Guilt with Truth

Emotions are not subject to truth. They just are. In order not to be led astray by emotions we must test them with truth or reality. Some parents may feel guilty for their lack of attention to the kids when they were young. Perhaps you over corrected them or put a career ahead of your parenting. Guilt over these things is just guilt. But once you go back and confess your failure and ask them for forgiveness, you are no longer guilty or worthy of blame (I John 1:9). Should you feel sad from time-to-time because of it? Yes, that's normal. But sadness and guilt are two very different emotions. Should you start repaying them for your past sin or compensate them for your lack of attention in years past? NO! It's foolish to think that if you started today and smothered them with attention or money you could repay them for the hurt. Friend, you will not live long enough to even put a dent in your debt. What is your child to do then? He has to grieve the loss just like you have to grieve your losses in life.

I put my father in an alcoholic rehabilitation program in his 70's. He had walked away from my mom, brothers and me 30 years earlier. I never had a dad as a teenager. Those losses were real. After my dad got out of the rehab hospital, I got him a job at a college where I worked and dad remained sober until he died at 89. Did those twenty years of good fellowship make up for all the lost years? No. But I biblically honored my dad and took care of him in his declining years.

Your kids may approach us like victims with all the entitlements victims believe they have. From their perceived or real losses they may attempt to put you on a guilt trip and to manipulate you. If you have confessed your past failures to the Lord and received His forgiveness (I John 1:9) and confessed this to your kids, you are no longer worthy of blame. Your kids will not be able to manipulate you if you are secure in your forgiveness from the Lord.

If your kids get angry because you failed to grant their rights as entitled victims, so be it. Unhealthy anger is designed to do at least one of three things: to change you, to control you or to manipulate you. If you believe it is your duty to control their anger by your compliance, you have assumed a responsibility that is not yours. Self-control is the fruit of the Holy Spirit, not the result of your compliance (Gal. 5:22, 23). Their tantrums are designed to change, control and manipulate you. It is totally about them now, not you. Some will use threats of abandonment or withdraw your exposure to your grandchildren. We will address grandchild issues in chapter 10.

Withdrawal of love and fellowship or any contact to punish you for not continuing to fund their irresponsibility, only reveals the deep emotional needs in them. Your response should be, "That is your choice but we hope and pray that you do not choose to cut off our relationship." If that fear is one of your hot buttons that sets you off into irresponsible behavior, it is up to you to get appropriate counsel and get to the root of that hot button. Usually it is an unresolved issue in your own birth family.

Guard Against Sibling Resentment

In your efforts to rectify a past failure with one of your kids, if you dole out money or privilege to the exclusion of his siblings, be prepared for jealousy and resentment. One adult child may cause a drain on the family's estate for drug rehabilitation or extensive counseling. You may have to help him and his family to get on their feet as a result of bad choices. You would be wise to keep track of all those expenses and keep the other siblings informed of what you are doing. Explain to them that what was spent on the rehabilitated sibling will be deducted from his part of the estate.

The siblings may choose to split the estate equally but that should be their decision. As much as possible, avoid an opportunity for the siblings to be resentful, jealous or accuse you of favoritism. God is just and shows no partiality (Acts 10:34). You need to be a just parent, free from partiality.

This is like the brother of the prodigal son who complained to his father that he had been faithful and look at all his wayward brother had done. He resented what his father was now doing for his prodigal son. The wise father reminded the older brother that all that he had now belonged to him. The estate settlement was fair, even though one of the sons received his portion of the estate early and squandered all of it (Luke 15:11-32).

Reward Positive Efforts

Linda and I were driving an old Volkswagen over a mountain pass between Los Angeles and Bakersfield, California when I was in graduate school in the late 60's. Gradually our transmission would not shift and we had to coast down the mountain and get it towed to a dealership. We finally reached Linda's parents' home in Hayward, California, just across the bay from San Francisco. Later that night Linda's father came into our room and dropped $500 down with the comment, "There was a time we needed some help too," and walked out of the room.

Linda taught school and I was a part-time pastor in a small rural church while I attended seminary. Finances were tight but we purposed to stay within our means and pay our bills. We focused on doing the next right thing financially. Linda's father was a frugal businessman, but he also knew the wisdom of rewarding those who were making an effort to be responsible. Years later, he asked how we were paying for my doctoral studies. He saw the sacrifice we were making and without asking he said, "Mom and I want to finish paying for the program." What a shock! Linda's parents were governed by at least two principles related to finances and their children; one, reward sacrificial efforts; and two, invest some of the estate in their kids now so they can enjoy them benefiting from it.

Children cannot develop responsibility if parents automatically reward their behaviors, especially negative ones. However, balance this with the opportunity to encourage the adult child financially who is doing all that he can. This is one occasion where it would be appropriate to share your financial resources with them. The Apostle Paul pointed out to the Corinthian church, "Children are not responsible to save up for their parents, but parents for their children" (2 Cor. 12:14b). Parents have worked hard and are usually in a better position to give because their basic needs are met and now they can help their children get a head start in life.

Respond Wisely to Your Kids' Crises

One of the most common problems in parenting is the over-reaction to an adult child's crisis in life. A crisis situation has a way of blinding individuals to their alternatives. Under pressure, the options and alternatives are usually overlooked. What usually happens is that the parent internalizes the kids' problems as their own and fails to remember these are the kids' issues or problems.[93] It is not a matter of not being concerned. That's normal. But once you become overly involved, you lose your perspective and potentially start making poor decisions with them. It is important to get some outside counsel yourself to remain balanced.

Too many parents make the mistake of trying to deal with their kids' crises without reaching out to others who have gone through similar experiences and learning from them what worked or didn't work. By not availing themselves of this help, parents often lose themselves while trying to save their children. In fact, some older couples end up divorcing after expending all their energies trying to help their adult children and failing to nurture their own relationship.[94] This is where it is crucial that you do the next *right* thing. If you just do the "next thing", it is usually impulsive, lacks wisdom and the results are less than desirable.

Over-emotional reactions may reveal a need for you to process your own past stuff that may be clouding your present judgment. Get appropriate help to clear that up so you can be more effective with your grown kids. This may have been one of many reasons Jesus counseled us to first remove the speck (issue) in our own eye (life) so we can see clearly to deal with the issues in our brothers' (or kids') lives (Matt. 7:1-5). Your issues may include the presence of guilt, fear, shame, depression, loneliness, rejection and past mistakes. One symptom of unresolved issues is a feeling of guilt if you enjoy yourself while your children are in crisis. Becoming emotionally obsessed with their problems can result in your becoming emotionally exhausted to the point you are no longer able to help at all.[95]

Ask Before You Loan

You may have worked hard all your life and reduced or even eliminated debt. Now you have some financial resources that you don't need immediately but your adult child does. You may not be in a position to give away a significant amount of money that you will need later, but you are open to making a short term loan. Here are some questions to consider before loaning a large amount money.

1. Are they utilizing the resources they have wisely? If you make this loan, will it be used wisely?

2. Is request for a want or a need? Delayed gratification is one sign of maturity. It means delaying pleasure. Without delayed gratification your child will not accept the responsibility to work through a problem. Be sure to define the need and assure yourself it is genuine.[96]

3. Will this help foster responsibility or irresponsibility in their life? Granting all our kids' requests without attaching conditions, stipulations of some sort of payback, either material or behaviorally, will have little effect on the child's future actions.[97]

4. Have they developed a pattern of needing to be bailed out from time to time? If you bail them out every time they have problems, you are taking them out of God's school of higher education and preventing them from learning important lessons. When you start to withdraw a drug (i.e. money) there are usually some serious side effects from the withdrawal, i.e. anger, hurt, feeling betrayed. The adult child will only grow up when he learns that the rewards of adulthood exceed the rewards of being dependent.

5. Am I prepared to act in a Christ-like way if the adult child reacts in a negative way over a "no" answer? You are not responsible for his response. Reassure them of your love. Do not argue with them. Remain pleasant even in the face of a bad response. Be sure you are clear about your reasons whether they agree or not. Technically, you do not owe them an explanation about why you will not do something that is not your responsibility.

6. Do you have all the facts? The time to get them is before you loan the money, not after.

7. Have you taken time to pray about it and to think it through? This will give you and your mate time to talk it through and come to mutual agreement. It is imperative that you both agree because you are one flesh before the Lord (Gen. 2:24). It is more difficult to achieve this when it involves a step parent or step adult child. If you are a widow, please consult a trusted Christian advisor.

8. Are you jeopardizing your own security by granting the gift or loan? Jesus had to remind His disciples they were always going to have people in need regardless how much they gave (Matt. 26:11).

9. Are you making a loan that would not be made by a bank? If they have been turned down, why? If it is a loan, are they really able to pay it back or are they just going deeper in the financial hole?

10. Are you willing to write the gift or loan off and not demand payment if they don't pay it back? Do not make the loan if it has the potential of jeopardizing your future relationships.

The Issue is Not the Issue

In most conflicts, the issue is not the issue. Just like the iceberg, ninety percent of the source of conflicts over money is really beneath the surface, unseen. Nothing reveals the submerged roots of past hurts, jealousies, fears, rejection, favoritism, greed, covetousness and selfishness like the issue of money and possessions, especially that of the parents.

The Apostle Paul plunged beneath the surface of the money issue and declared it was not money but the love of money that was the cause of all kinds of evil (I Tim. 6:10). Even Jesus identified the submerged motives of a man who yelled out of a crowd, "Tell my brother to share the inheritance with me." To which Jesus responded, "Take heed and beware of all covetousness for one's life does not consist in the abundance of things he possesses" (Luke 12:13-15). You may not be able to readily see what lies beneath the surface of your grown children's issues with you and your money. Ask God to search your heart to see if you have been fair, just, mature, wise, without favoritism and partiality. God is faithful to grant you the wisdom you request when you are confronted with making a financial choice with your adult children (James 1:5-8).

In many cases it is a lot easier to handle your adult children's needs and requests when it just involves them. What do you do when your decisions could adversely affect your grandchildren? How do you grandparent wisely? We'll need the wisdom of Solomon to address this in the next chapter.

CHAPTER 9

Points to Ponder

1. Resist falling for the entitlement trap.
2. Separate logic from emotion.
3. Distinguish between affordability and responsibility.
4. Remember you are responsible to God for the stewardship of your assets.
5. Stop all enabling practices.
6. Encourage them to learn to provide for themselves.
7. Reduce subsidies slowly.
8. Test your guilt feelings with truth and reality.
9. Guard against sibling resentment.
10. Reward their positive efforts.
11. Respond wisely to your kid's crises.
12. Get the facts before you loan money.
13. Realize their current issue may not be the real issue.

CHAPTER 9

Dispense Resources Wisely

Small Group Questions

1. What entitlement traps have you experienced and how did you deal with them? What was the outcome of your actions? What would you do differently and why?

2. How have you had to distinguish between affordability and being responsible? How did you learn to do that? Share one lesson you learned when you had to make that distinction.

3. What questions have you asked yourself before you have dispensed financial resources to your grown kids? How did you come up with those questions?

4. Have you ever sought advice from a friend, pastor or counselor regarding dispensing resources to your grown kids? What advice did you receive and how helpful was it?

5. What experience did you have that prepared you to handle your finances?

6. Describe a time when you had to step back and let your grown children learn some hard financial lessons. What kind of personal struggles did you go through to allow it to happen?

7. What struggles as a couple did you have to go through in dealing with your grown kids' financial issues? How did you deal with it if you did not come to an agreement?

8. In what ways did you train your kids to "fish" or even be willing to put the line in the water? How did you motivate them? What would you do differently if you had to do it all over again?

9. How have you had to address your own emotions of guilt, fear, shame, disappointments and regrets regarding your grown kids? What scripture did you apply personally during these difficult times?

10. How have you had to find that delicate balance between your adult children regarding fairness, impartiality and resisting favoritism? How have you handled unfair accusations from your grown kids?

11. How has God used the issue of favoritism to reveal deeper needs in your relationships with your kids?

12. What biblical "tools" have you had to use to deal with sibling resentment? Where does it stand now?

13. In what ways have you been able to tangibly reward the efforts of your grown kids who have been financially responsible?

14. Describe your own personal struggles watching your kids go through the financial growing pains of adulthood. What did God teach you through it?

15. What kind of check list or criteria did you have before you responded to a request for financial assistance? How has that list worked for you?

CHAPTER 10

Grandparent Wisely

In 1992 Linda and I were invited to be in on the delivery of our first grandchild. What a memorable experience! I was not re-living my wife giving birth to DeeDee, our first child. We both were watching DeeDee give birth to our first grandchild. Very few experiences in life can rival that. Linda and I knew our lives as a couple would change drastically. We now had a whole new set of responsibilities and sphere of influence.

Understand Your New Potential for Influence

Grandparents are the heart of the extended family. We refer to them as the patriarchs of the clan and with that new role comes responsibilities and potential for influence. One of those new areas of influence is to be a faith role model to your grandchildren. You become their rock of stability. When everything else is churned up in the world of change, their eyes can look to you as the family anchor.

You have an incredible opportunity to offer a listening ear which tends not to be judgmental. Grandchildren seem to find it easier to open up about their problems and discuss issues and with grandparents. You learned long ago that it is more important to listen and make an effort to understand than it is to quickly offer solutions (James 1:19). You have the time to listen with fewer distractions. You now are freer to offer unconditional love, kindness and insightful understanding.

The writer of Hebrews lists another major influence you offer. "Encourage one another daily while it is called today." Then he adds the reason, "lest any of you be hardened though the deceitfulness of sin" (Heb. 3:13). Our grandkids are bombarded with lies in our culture that are designed to destroy them. We can be their cheerleaders to do the next right thing by identifying and correcting the lies they are being led to believe, even the lies they believe about themselves.

When our granddaughter has a volleyball tournament in town, we get a call. She wants us to come and watch. More than that, she wants to hear us cheer her on. It can also be compared to watching them give a musical performance, and from the balcony, we enthusiastically cheer and applaud them. We become their balcony people of encouragement. Why is that so important to them? Simple. We hold the important privilege of being the family patriarch, a high position of value. When they hear cheers from us, it has extra special meaning to them. There are very few relationships that hold a greater potential for mutual pleasure, affirmation and influence than a loving grandparent-grandchild bond.[98] By the same token, our grandchildren are likened to a crown of glory in our senior years (Prov. 17:6).

A source of potential influence is our ability to give spiritual guidance. We have learned what works and what doesn't work in life. We have fought the demons of doubt, fear, rejection, loss, disappointment and have come to the conclusion that God is faithful. It is one thing to read about it; it is a totally different thing to experience it. Job admitted after the major losses in his life, "I have heard of You by the hearing of the ear … but now my eye sees You" (Job 42:4).

Dr. Roy Zuck commented on Job's new insight, "This thrilling view of God, probably spiritual insight, not physical vision, deepened his perspective and appreciation of God."[99] It was insight gained through a difficult time that gave Job new understanding. That is exactly what you have to offer your grandkids. Their parents have probably not walked with God as long as you have and have not learned the deep lessons from life experience. If you are a new believer, you are now able to re-evaluate your life and pass on the new insights you have gained. God never wastes life experience on anyone, if we are willing to learn from it.

With this privileged position as spiritual guide, you also assume the position as their role model. Shauna Smith has rightly said, 'Modeling is the most powerful form of influence."[100] The Apostle Peter reminded the elders of the church that with their position they were also to prove to be role models of Christ's church (I Peter 5:3). What do you do if you have not been a role model in the past? Share with your grandkids that you have failed in that responsibility, but you now fully intend, with God's grace, to change. That one act of humility can restore you to a powerful place of influence.

Acknowledge Who the Parent is

With the incredible privilege that is ours, we have to take a step back and remind ourselves daily that we are the grandparents, not the parents. Many unnecessary battles have been fought between parents and grandparents as to who makes the final decisions about the children.[101] When we continue to view our grown children as kids, we will talk to them as kids even if they have children of their own. That, then, sets the grandparents up to assume the role of parents in their grandkids' lives. God will never judge you as a parent to your grandchildren. As immature and irresponsible as your grown kids may act, God will judge them as adults, therefore, you must view them as God does, as adults.

When grandparents assume parental roles, huge loyalty issues and power struggles often take place between the adults.[102] It is in your circle of responsibility to acknowledge your kids are the primary care-givers of your grandchildren and are entitled to have the last word. Therefore never overstep the rights and authority of the parents, except in emergencies where physical, emotional or sexual abuse is present. Parents do not have absolute power. They are subject to civil law and to God (Rom. 13).

One practical way to acknowledge who is the parent is to consult with them before you give or loan money to the grandchildren. Avoid making extravagant plans or giving major advice without first gaining the approval of the parents. If you want to take the grandkids to Hawaii, fine! But first, consult the parents. They may have plans they have not shared with you or there may be a serious discipline issue they are trying to address, and that special trip at this time would not be appropriate.

A hard area to respect is that of discipline. As difficult as it may be, you must respect the parents' wishes regarding discipline. They may be too strict and they may view you to be too lenient or vice versa, but discipline is in their circle of responsibility, not yours. Here is where you can have an adult-to-adult talk and clarify what each of you expects to take place when you have the grandchildren. Avoid telling the grandkids, "You may get away with this at your house but you will not do that in my home." It is more appropriate to clarify to the kids what is expected at grandma and grandpa's home. If the parents fail to clarify it for you, then you merely state that at your home this is how we behave and avoid verbally comparing it to their home. Unfavorable comparison drastically undermines the parents. It is appropriate that any physical discipline that may need to be administered should be done by the parents. Serious infractions should be reported to the parents and leave the choice of the discipline with them. It is crucial that you have a clear understanding of what the parents can expect from you while the children are in your care.

We have house rules in our home that differ from our grown kids. If the grandkids are in our care they can choose to eat or not to eat the meal that has been prepared. If they choose not to eat, they get no snacks, desserts or treats later. We do make a special effort to serve kid-friendly meals when they are with us - no liver and onions. Nor do we try to make them health food converts. One evening our nine-year-old grandson started to cry because he did not like what was served even though he had liked it three weeks earlier. We asked him to excuse himself from the table and go into the guest room if he was going to continue to cry. He was not told he could not cry, nor was he shamed for crying. We told him we would prefer him to stay at the table because we liked his company.

He chose to leave. A few minutes later he peeked around the corner and asked if he could come back to the table. We said, "Yes," and that we missed him and we were happy he chose to be with us. Neither he nor his siblings did that again.

The word discipline is related to the word disciple. To the degree you disciple, you will have less need to discipline. Yet, to the degree you fail to disciple, teach or illustrate, to that same degree you will have more need to discipline. We view every visit with our grandkids as an opportunity to disciple, not just make them behave. That is a choice you have to make. The grandkids may live with different house rules than you have. These differences in parenting styles could create problems in parent and adult-child relationships but they do not have to. We need to accept the difference and not criticize the difference. Shauna Smith offers some very good advice on this point. "As a general rule to minimize dissention; unless you are asked advice, think hard and seriously before you criticize someone else's parenting style as long as the way they are handling the children does not directly affect you or qualify as child abuse."[103] Smith further states, "Remember though, that one of the best ways to teach your adult child anything about parenting is by example. If you are getting a hostile response from them, you may not be acting as effectively as a parent as you think, and any advice you offer will be undermined by your own actions."[104]

Adjust to Your Children's Divorce

When one of my brothers went through a divorce it was devastating to my mother. She had a very deep relationship with her daughter-in-law. I can still see the pain in her face when the topic came up. Divorce is especially hard for those who are in their sixties, seventies and older. There was less divorce in that generation and it was usually the result of adultery or abuse. Today our grown kids just say, "The spark is not there anymore" or "He's just not as exciting anymore." This attitude seems foreign to the older generation who grew up with a "for richer, for poorer" mindset.

Your first task is to work through the disappointment and the loss of an intact marriage. You may consider getting some professional help to work through all the new issues and relationship changes that the divorce has brought about. Use this time to deepen your own relationship with the Lord and tap into the comfort that He so generously offers (2 Cor. 1:4). Your next task is to accept the reality you can't fix the adult children's marriage, even though it is your first knee-jerk reaction to do so. Usually, by the time we get the news, it's pretty much a done deal. Plus, your kids may not want you to repair the marriage. That's the hard part. You can love, demonstrate genuine care, hug them, earnestly pray for them and offer a listening ear. Avoid assuming the blame for the divorce if you were not intrusive in their marriage. If both spouses invite your input, do not hesitate to share it based on the ground rules we discussed in chapter three.

When you are with the grandkids make a point to re-assure them that your feelings have not changed toward them and that you still deeply love them. It is not your responsibility to explain, defend, excuse or justify your adult children's behavior. You should share the least amount of information regarding their parents' divorce. Remember, it is the parents' responsibility to answer those questions, not yours. What if this is not possible? Then give as little and as age-appropriate information as possible. Stay in your role of being as loving, caring, re-assuring and supportive as you can.[105]

Resist running down either parent. You have to acknowledge obvious wrongs when forced to. You can acknowledge a child's pain and comfort them. Build up or reinforce as much love and respect for their parents as possible. There is a very good reason for this. Their future success may be based on their ability to honor their hurtful parent with respect even when they do not deserve it (Eph. 6:2, 3).

Sadly, my mother did all she could to get me to hate my dad most of my adult life. Thirty years later I was put in a position of having to take care of my dad until he died. However, my mom's bitterness did not change my mind about my dad. On the contrary, it did make it hard to respect her. Injecting bitterness in others can backfire on you. Remember, you are the patriarch of the family and others are going to look to you for their cues about how to respond to the ex-spouse. If you criticize the ex, you will find others will too. This will deeply hurt the grandkids when they hear about it. Those you are criticizing are their mom and dad, for better or worse. Your task is, if possible, to preserve the relationship with the divorced spouse that is related to you.

The Scripture does not allow an exception to the command to honor your father and mother (Eph. 6:2,3) even when they are wrong. It is an attitude of the heart. Honor as adults does not mean obedience or agreement with them. I could, in honor, share with my mother how I felt about what she was doing, but I did it with grace and respect. However, she never stopped criticizing my father until the day she died.

As an adult you can choose to maintain a relationship with the ex-spouse because you probably invested a lot of relational energy into him/her. He/she is still a parent of your grandchildren. Avoid comparing the new spouse with the old spouse, especially to the grandchildren. You have to respect them both, even if you dislike the new spouse. God demonstrated His love toward us while we were still sinners (Rom. 5:8). You may need to consider keeping your contact with the ex-spouse to a minimum in order to reduce potential friction. You are totally free as an adult to choose to see your adult child with or without their new spouse. You have to allow them the same freedom to accept or reject either option. You don't have to have a close relationship with everyone concerned, but you will want to be open to making it as good as it can be under the circumstances, while reflecting a Christ-like attitude.[106]

With divorce the ideal is broken. It will never be the same. We do not like change or loss. Now we have to face both and grieve the loss of the breakup. The grandchildren did not divorce, their parents did. They will only have one set of birth parents. Our task is to be a healing agent in a very painful hurt. Be a source of stability, emotional support and in some cases, financial help to the grandkids.

Develop a Relationship with Step Grandchildren

When your kids divorce, it is a given they will remarry. Eighty percent of divorced people remarry. You have to accept their decision to remarry and seek to relate positively and biblically with the new mate. It's their choice. Ignoring this reality will not foster good relationships. It is one thing to have to build a relationship with your grown child's new spouse. It is still another thing to build a relationship with the new step grandkids that the spouse brings to the marriage. Remember, the grandchildren did not want this divorce any more than you did. In reality, only the adults got re-married, not the kids. It's tough on them, too. They have to choose to make the best of the new situation, just like you do.

Your task is to choose to relate to your child's step children in as gracious and accepting way as possible. You will probably not feel as close or love them as much as your own grandkids. That's all right. Step parents rarely love step children like they do their own birth children. Accept the fact that they already have another set of grandparents. You are set number three. They are not related to you by blood. They may have already bonded with the other set of grandparents. You may be an unwelcome addition. How should you respond?

You cannot force your step grandchildren to accept you or even like you. When their parents divorced and remarried, it dashed all hopes that their birth parents' marriage would ever be restored. Their anger can run deep and be turned on you undeservingly. Remind yourself it is not about you. Comfort them in their loss by acknowledging that you understand how hurtful this whole thing is to them. Avoid lectures and make an effort to show compassion and understanding. That just might open the door of their hearts toward you. As an adult you must be as cordial, friendly and Christ-like as possible to them. They may not want to call you grandpa or grandma. That's their choice! They may want to call you

Mr. or Mrs. until you have won their hearts. Reassure them it is okay with you to be addressed either way.

On a serious note, you must report to your adult child any signals of mistreatment of the grandchildren by the step parent. If he is not mentally or emotionally able to confront an abusive mate, you may need to contact the appropriate social agencies to intercede. This could deeply damage your relationship with your adult child and his new spouse, but the health and safety of the children are more important than your relationship with your irresponsible kids.

When I had to report a step dad to the Department of Family Services for sexually abusing his step daughter, they removed him from the home. The birth mother could not live with the court restriction prohibiting her husband from being in the home at the same time as her daughter. She could not choose between the two so she took her life. Never forget that when the abused grandchild reaches adulthood, he may be more bitter toward the parent or grandparent that knew what was going on and did not stop it than he is toward the perpetrator.

Trust the Lord for Strength to Raise your Grandchildren

My father was raised by much older parents. I learned later that he had been adopted by these senior citizens. Then I learned the truth behind his adoption. My dad's biological parents were in the entertainment industry. His mom got pregnant and they did not want a child to complicate their careers so they gave him up for adoption. These senior parents raised both my dad and his birth father because they could not have any children of their own. My dad commented years later that he felt his adoptive parents had no business raising him, implying that they were too old.

But today there is a growing number of grandparents who feel obligated to assume full-time financial, physical and emotional responsibility for their grandchildren.[107] Divorce, death, abuse, addictions, teenage pregnancy, chronic unemployment or sheer abandonment are just a few of the reasons grandparents find themselves raising their grandchildren. These recycled parents, who find themselves assuming the role and responsibility of the biological parents, are often bewildered and even depressed by how their lives have changed. They looked forward to spoiling the grandkids but never expected to assume the primary role of raising them. The empty nest refills. The guest room gets converted to a nursery. Retirement dreams are postponed or forfeited. They watch their savings drain. They may feel powerless, frustrated, resentful, alienated, guilty and punished.[108]

Why do we become recycled parents? One reason is that we feel guilty and responsible for not accomplishing something while raising our own kids.[109] I have warned dysfunctional parents who do not raise their children to be healthy adults that they may end up raising their grandchildren. Sadly, this often becomes reality. Every parent has failed sometime along the parenting road but that is a poor reason to assume the responsibility to raise their grandkids. Guilt instead of love is a poor motivator. Sooner or later, the guilt will turn to anger and later resentment with disastrous results.

Most grandparents who are faced with this decision feel trapped. Your first task is to challenge that statement with the facts. You are not trapped. You have adult choices. The children can be put in foster care or adopted by someone other than yourself. You may strongly react that no grandkid of yours is going to be put in foster care or "given away." Okay! Then be intellectually honest and admit that you are going to make an adult choice between difficult options. Are any of the choices good ones? Are they ideal choices? No. So remind yourself that the ideal family is broken. The parents can't raise their children, so you choose to raise them yourself or allow them to go into foster care or be adopted by someone else. You are not trapped!

This is a great opportunity to tap into every resource available to you and the grandkids. Find a support group of other grandparents and mutually share each others' burdens (Gal. 6:2). They may know of resources that you are not aware of. Check out your church, community and government agencies. This is a growing phenomenon and you are not alone. Tap into the deep resources God will give you. View your task as a long term discipleship course. You just may be the people that will rescue them from disaster and, in turn, disciple them to be godly adults.

Share Your Resources Wisely with Returnees and their Kids

When adult children are overdue to leave the nest that is one level of stress. When they return to the nest to prepare to leave again or to stay long term, that is a little higher stress. But when an adult child returns to the nest with her kids, the parents' stress level skyrockets. Much of what applies to grown kids living at home or returning home can be applied here, but now you have additional stressful issues.

Focus on God's Plan

The presence of your grandchild and parent living in your home does not change God's plan for your adult child to grow up and be a mature, healthy adult. Remind yourself that they are adults and are ultimately responsible for their own lives and their children's lives before God. Your grown kids are not there to be re-parented, but they should be required to seek outside counsel from one who is experienced in adult child issues. Your role of being a parent ended. You are now a mentor or guide with the full understanding that they are free to take or reject your advice. Do not revert to a parent-child relationship. That foolish step could thwart God's plan for them to grow up and to put away their childish ways (I Cor. 13:11).

Focus on Circles of Responsibility

The Apostle Paul summarized a volume of information on personal responsibility in one short verse, "If possible as much as it lies with you, be at peace with all men" (Rom. 12:18). In our final chapter we will define how to resolve conflicts biblically by identifying what is in your circle of responsibility. Here I strongly urge you to identify what needs to be done around the home and who is going to do it; more specifically, the child care and discipline.

The first important principle is to never over-rule the parents or criticize their abilities or decisions, especially in front of the children. You may have to take a deep breath, then, ask your adult child when you can meet with them privately. If they refuse to work with you based on a former agreement that 'this is how we agreed to discuss issues', then other steps should be taken which will be addressed later. Every parent is sensitive about their parenting, but certain rights have been forfeited when they moved back into your home. You may have to meet regularly to work on, adjust and clarify the current needs and review the long-range goals. If you just let things happen, you will fall into the trap of being a reactor instead of being proactive. You do not have an ideal living situation. It will take a lot of hard work to keep from wanting to kill each other.

Utilize Outside Resources

Just because your adult child's family has moved home, it does not mean you are now totally responsible for everything. They are still part of the community at large even though they are living in your home. Utilize the resources in your area like the church, city, county, non-profit and religious agencies. The community has set up these resources to help. They will help reinforce that you are not totally responsible or alone. If your adult child's pride is preventing them from tapping into those resources, then we are dealing with a spiritual issue that needs to be addressed biblically and spiritually. God gives a lot of grace to those who are able to humble themselves (I Peter 5:5b). God will resist the proud and, by default, not provide the needed resources. Most of us have paid a lot of taxes over the years to the government for many of these needed services. They are designed to meet these legitimate needs. If your adult child is not open to change his thinking and cooperate with mutually agreed upon plans and goals and utilize outside resources, all your heroic efforts of sacrifice will not make a significant difference over the long haul. As an adult, your grown child can choose to walk away from your parental support in spite of all the love you have demonstrated to him in tangible ways. At this point, it is not about you. It is all about him.

Initiate Responsible Love

When your adult child chooses to stay and not cooperate by following through with mutually agreed upon plans, then it's time for the parents to initiate "responsible love." I prefer this designation rather than "tough love." You are not getting tough; you are in a loving way allowing him to feel the full weight of the responsibility of his choices. When they reject you and your services, it is important to allow him the choice of experiencing his own resources, whether it's his friend or government agencies. This is not cruelty, as he may assert. It is the next step of accepting full responsibility which he may not like. Calling you "cruel" is his way of shifting blame and focus off of his poor choices and his sense of entitlement. Your task is to remain gentle, loving and firm and not resort to anger. Do not wait until you are angry before you choose to do the next right thing. Be guided by God's Spirit, not your selfish anger. You must now allow him to register in the school of hard knocks. Unfortunately, most of his classmates are probably fools and a grief to their parents (Prov. 17:25).

How do you know if you are taking appropriate steps? One confirmation is when your adult children respond to you in anger, tantrums, shaming, manipulation and guilt trips. They are attempting to make this all about you while totally ignoring that it is really all about them and their distorted world view of entitlements. Their fear has kicked in. This is good because part of adulthood is facing fear and identifying the object of fear and dealing with it. Now they have the opportunity to include God in their thinking as the ultimate supplier of their needs, not you (Phil. 4:19). There is no long-term change without experiencing the depth of long-term pain. When adult children neither consider nor seem to care about the effects on you as their children's grandparents, remind yourself that you are no longer responsible for the actions of your adult children.[110]

What is a biblical strategy to resolve the conflicts you face with your grown children? Is there one strategy you can live with even if your kids do not cooperate? God has dealt with conflict in His creation ever since Adam and Eve. He has four simple principles that work each time they are utilized. In chapter 11, we will explore these strategies.

CHAPTER 10

Points to Ponder

1. Understand your new potential for influence.
2. Acknowledge who the parent is.
3. Consult parents before giving large gifts or making lavish plans with the grandkids.
4. Disciple more; discipline less.
5. Adjust to your children's divorce.
6. Never run down either of the parents to the grandkids.
7. Preserve your relationship with your divorced kids.
8. Develop a relationship with your step grandchildren.
9. Trust the Lord as you raise your grandchildren.
10. Share your resources wisely.
11. Focus on God's plan.
12. Focus on circles of responsibility.
13. Utilize outside resources.
14. Initiate responsible love.

CHAPTER 10

Grandparent Wisely

Small Group Questions

1. What are practical ways you have influenced your grandchildren?

2. When have you had to remind yourself that you are not the parent of your grandchildren? What have you done differently because of that realization?

3. What kind of conflict have you experienced over the discipline issues with your grandchildren? How did you deal with it and what was the response?

4. How have you handled the difference between your house rules and your adult children's house rules? What have you done that was effective and what do you wish you had done differently?

5. What are some creative ways that were helpful in disciplining your grandkids? What worked and what didn't work?

6. What adjustments did you face when your adult children divorced? How did it change your relationship with them, the grandkids and the other set of in-laws? What helped you the most while going through that transition?

7. What difficult situations did you face in talking with your grandkids about their parents' divorce?

8. What transitions do you expect would have to take place with new step grandchildren?

9. What challenges can grandparents expect to face in raising their grandchildren? What biblical principles would be helpful to assist in this major undertaking?

10. How have you personally dealt with failures you have observed in your adult children? What scripture would be helpful to help process this?

11. What are some practical tips for grandparents whose adult children and grandkids move into their home? What biblical principles must be observed to make the best of a difficult situation?

12. What are your guiding principles in relating to your grandchildren and their parents? What have you had to adjust over the years?

13. What is the best advice you could give to new grandparents?

CHAPTER 11

Resolve Conflicts Biblically

That late afternoon call from Robert and Bev often replays in my mind when I meet with other frustrated parents of adult children. As they pour out their hearts, I can hear the same nagging question that Robert and Bev asked. It's the same question we ask ourselves when we are in a relationship that is jarred by conflict. It's only four words, "What can we do?" Why do they ask? Because whatever they are doing is not working. It is followed by the question, "Who should do it?" God illustrates four principles over and over in His Word that, if followed, will answer those questions and bring a conflict to a healthy solution.

The disciples handled the first major conflict that arose in the early church using these principles. The Greek-speaking Jews felt their widows were being neglected in the distribution of food by the local Aramaic-speaking Jews (Acts 6:1). This is the first step in resolving a conflict, to identify what is actually taking place. Apparently the complaint was legitimate.

Next, the apostles quickly defined their responsibility. Some may have suggested they take on the task of distributing the food to all the widows to ensure the Greek widows were amply served. However, the apostles made it clear that their circle of responsibility was to minister the Word of God and to spend time in prayer (Acts 6:2,4) and not assume the food distribution responsibility. Instead, they put forth a plan that was acceptable to all. They assigned to seven Greek-speaking Jews the job of overseeing the distribution.

This second step in working through a conflict is to assign to each person what he is responsible for. After identifying the seven men and assigning their responsibilities, the apostles laid hands on them signifying their authority to carry it out (Acts 6:6).

The third aspect of God's pattern for resolving conflict is to assume what has been assigned. The seven men were selected but they had to agree to assume the responsibility. Apparently they went right to work because the tension was reduced and the young church was free to spread the Word of God throughout Jerusalem. Stephen, one of the seven, was controlled by God's Spirit and full of wisdom, faith, grace and power (Acts 6:8). He demonstrated these evidences of God's grace in addition to fulfilling his responsibility in the daily distribution to the widows.

The fourth aspect of God's plan to bring a healthy resolution to the conflict is to fulfill what is in your circle of responsibility. These the same four principles can be used to bring a healthy conclusion to a conflict with your grown kids or greatly reduce tension between them and you. Maturity is not the ability to eliminate problems; rather it is the ability to work out difficulties when they arise. These four keys, if applied, can help you do just that.

1. Identify what actually happened.
2. Assign responsibility for all the parts of the conflict.
3. Assume responsibility for the assigned parts.
4. Fulfill what is in your circle of responsibility.

Identify What Happened

Abandon the Comfort of Denial

The very first step in honestly identifying what is taking place in a conflict is to abandon the false security of denial. Most conflicts with grown children did not start when they turned 18 or 21. Often there were patterns of denial that assisted them in avoiding past issues. Denial is a defense strategy we use to pretend that what is true is not really true. It is a false reality to protect us from facing things about ourselves or our kids that we could not deal with in the past or present. It protects from a reality that is too painful to think about. It is our protective shield.[111] Nowhere does it say that problems with grown children must be ignored until they are intolerable, overwhelming, unwieldy and damaging. The fear of rejection, abandonment, anger, fighting and withholding love, fellowship and time with the grandchildren can keep you locked in the prison of denial.

God has a different perspective on denial. Christian denial is denying God access to a hurt or conflict that He wants to heal for your benefit and for His glory (Matt. 5:16). The consequence of denial is enormous because it limits and distorts our perception of the issues and of God's purpose for them. Breaking through denial, whether yours or your adult children's, will give you a better possibility for an improved quality of life.

God Only Gives Grace for Truth

Jesus did not minister to others only with grace or only with truth. The Apostle John made it clear that Jesus came to us with both grace and truth (John 1:14). God will rarely grant you grace to deal with a difficult relationship unless it is dealt with in truth and reality. God does not give grace for denial. He only grants grace for the truth. He expects truth to come from your innermost being (Psalm 51:6). Identifying the truth is the first step toward working through a conflict. Unfortunately, truth is the first casualty in a conflict.

The truth can be painful to face. You may have to acknowledge you were an over-protective, indulgent parent or your kids may have walked away from their faith, rejected your values, or not been responsible parents themselves. And just when you're ready to enjoy some well-earned retirement, your grandkids are dumped on you to raise or your single son returns home pulling a three-year-old behind him. Your married kids may always be in a financial crisis because they never learned to manage money. You've come to the point you don't even want to answer the phone.

You can do one of the most difficult things in a conflict, leave denial and face reality and you will be amazed what grace, mercy and comfort you will experience from God (II Cor. 1:4). You may have to admit you were critical, aloof, absent, selfish, over-indulgent, passive, abusive, demeaning, enmeshed, authoritarian, harsh, hypocritical, career driven, unapproachable, angry, bitter, proud, unforgiving, too strict, lenient, showed favoritism or failed as a role model. Now you have to face the reality that your adult children may be irresponsible, manipulative, emotionally dependent, adolescent in their thinking, lazy, immoral, irreligious, rebellious, disrespectful, helpless, under-motivated, users, abusers, selfish, purposeless, failures or relationship addicted.

You may find it hard to admit you were not perfect parent and your kids mirror that same imperfection. Now that they are grown, you can't change them. They are adults with all the rights, privileges and responsibilities of adults even though they may not act like it. It is difficult to come to grips with the reality that you still have the position of parent but your function has changed to mentor, guide or advisor. They can take or leave your advice. You are now the grandparent and not the parent of your grandchildren. The immature adult children have the last word over those grandkids that are the joy and delight of your heart.

You may not want to see the truth so that you won't have to experience the negative feelings behind the truth like guilt, shame, fear, anger, regret, sadness, hopelessness, rejection, betrayal, loss, pride, failure and being overwhelmed. It may be a struggle to see your face in the mirror of truth because there is a responsibility you do not want to fulfill. You may have to forgive even when you see no change in your child. Harder still, you may need to confess your wrongs and ask to be forgiven. You would stop blaming your kids and start taking responsibility for yourself and establish some healthy boundaries. This may mean you will have to say no even when it costs you a relationship and time with the grandkids. There may be a deeper reason you cannot walk out of the fog of denial into the light of truth. It is your motives. You may have been selfish, jealous, greedy, envious, manipulative or controlling. These motives may lurk behind your stubborn denial. Recall again what God demands before He participates in healthy conflict resolution – truth.

Take an Honest X-Ray

No medical doctor will perform surgery until he has taken a series of x-rays or MRIs to help him determine what to do. These x-rays also serve a benefit to the patient before any surgical procedure is undertaken. He may not believe his arm is broken, but when he sees the x-rays for himself, he will allow the doctor to put a cast on it. You may need to take a relational x-ray or inventory and list out the dynamics of the conflict before you will be convinced purposeful actions must be taken, and taken soon. Many times I have had parents list on one side of a piece of paper where they believe they are "AT" in the relationship and then, on the opposite side list where they would like to "BE". Usually where they would like to be is just the opposite of where they are.

If the adult children are in the counseling sessions with their parents, I simply have them add to the list. But I try to prevent anyone from designating who is doing what, they're just to list what is taking place. It's hard to do. If they start telling who is doing what, sometimes the honest sharing shuts down. When no names are listed with the negative items in the "AT" column then everyone is free to name the dynamics of the conflict. The following is a partial list of some of the most common "AT" issues in a conflict, then, look at their opposites and that is where they should "BE".

AT	BE
Abusive	Caring
Angry	Forgiven
Distrusting	Trusting
Insecure	Secure
Dependent	Independent
Controlling	Free
Rejected	Accepted
Fearful	Peaceful
Irresponsible	Responsible
Spender	Saver
Proud	Humble
Disrespectful	Respectful
Selfish	Generous
Hypocritical	Genuine
Demeaning	Honoring
Passive	Pro-active

This helps you to identify where you are "AT" in a conflict and where you want to "BE". The "AT" list sets you up for the next step which can be especially challenging.

Assign Responsibility for the Parts

One small verse, Romans 12:18, establishes the basis for the next important step. "If it is possible, as much as it depends on you, live peaceably with all men." The key phrase is "as much as it depends on you." We refer to this concept as circles of responsibility. The apostle does not say "live in peace as much as it depends on someone else." God makes it clear that you are to do everything you can in your circle of responsibility and pray it brings a peaceful end. But the Apostle Paul is not naive. Note the first four words of that verse, "If it is possible." He knows full well that you can do everything right in your circle of responsibility and it can still blow up in your face. Jesus did everything right and was killed. It is your task to identify what part of the conflict is your responsibility and then place it in your circle.

Who is Doing What?

When Bev and Robert came to see me they laid out a very bleak story. It had to do with their grown daughter. I took a yellow note pad and drew three separate circles and listed one person's name under each circle. Why did I draw three separate circles? Parents report that their problems with their grown kids are very complicated. In their minds, they draw one big circle and draw three smaller circles inside. It appears everyone is responsible for everything.

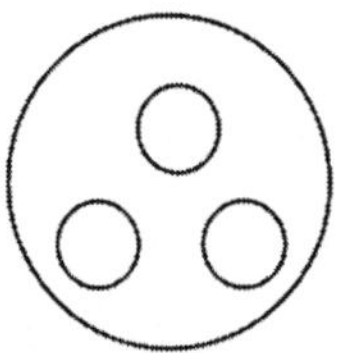

Our task is to draw a line from those three smaller circles to three separate circles outside the big circle. Once you separate out each person's circle and label it, then it becomes immediately clear who is responsible for what and who should do what. That answers our earlier question, "What can we (I) do?"

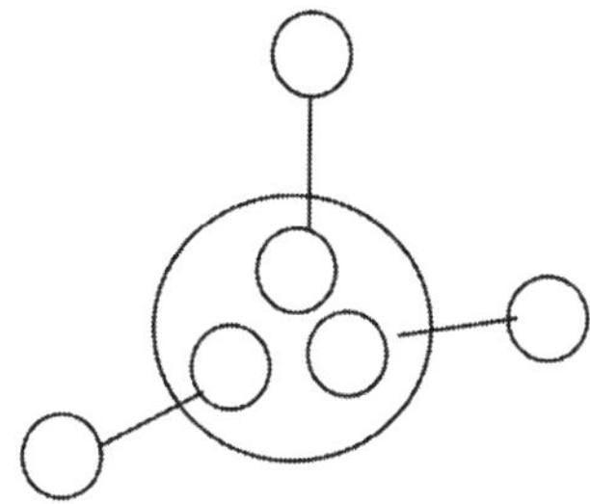

After reading Romans 12:18 to Robert and Bev, I asked a very simple question, "What is in your circle of responsibility?" They wanted to know what they could do about their daughter and her poor choices. I asked them to put in short sentences what they thought was happening as it relates to actions, words and attitudes.

Robert admitted he was hurt and angry. So we put hurt and anger in Robert's circle. Bev said she probably needed to add that to her circle, too. Who was responsible for spending the $10,000 inheritance and giving an account to God for how the money was spent? They gladly put that in their daughter's circle. Who tended to be controlling? Bev raised her hand, "Guilty as charged." She wrote that in her circle. Whose responsibility is it for skipping Bible college and going to California to pursue a husband? Who is responsible for that decision before God? The daughter won that one. Who has created a deep dependency by over-controlling? Who needed to let their daughter learn hard lessons of life? Without looking at each other, they both wrote "the need to let go" in their circles.

As we continued to address the fears, regrets, disappointments, shame, guilt, selfishness and many more issues, it became clear who was responsible for what. I, then, drew a fourth circle above their three circles and wrote "God" under that circle. I asked, "What is in God's circle of responsibility?" That was tough. Why? Because it is in His circle to convict, change, judge, discipline, reprove and order events that might lead to repentance. It was in Mom and Dad's circle to do the hard thing, to trust.

One of the temptations at this point is to attempt to shift blame which is an irresponsible technique to relieve yourself of guilt or accountability for your actions. Both parents owned up to being hurt, angry and bitter. They could have said, "If she had not done this, then, we would not be so angry." Question? Who is responsible for dealing with anger and bitterness? We are 100% responsible for our responses to those deep hurts. On the other hand, grief, sadness and disappointment are all normal responses to hurts like this.

The temptation is to shrink your circle to the size of a pea and inflate their circles to the size of a basketball. But God reverses this pattern. He said, first, deal with the log in your own eye, then, you can see clearly to take the splinter from your child's eye (Matt.7:5). As parents, we must take responsibility for the "logs" in our own sphere of influence and stop blaming our children for the bad relationship. Why? We are older and should be more mature. Our adult children are on the front end of life, still trying to learn. Our task is to create a good climate in which that learning can take place.[112] Taking this very humbling step of removing your own log may just open a closed door in your adult child's heart.

Assume Responsibility for the Assigned Parts

It is one thing to assign responsibility for one's wrong actions; it is quite another thing to assume what is assigned.

Assigning and assuming responsibility are two separate steps. You can tell a child to clean up his room. Later, you discover the room was not cleaned up. You assigned the task, but he did not assume the responsibility to fulfill the task.

At this point in the process I have asked many parents "Are you going to assume full responsibility for your own attitudes, actions and words?" I ask you the same question. Are you going to assume your responsibility regardless of what your grown children do? Are you waiting to take responsibility for your own stuff before God? Are you waiting for your adult children to change or take the first step? Who has more life experience and should have a greater measure of maturity under their belt?

At the same time, resist assuming your child's responsibility in order to make peace, to avoid guilt feelings, to gain acceptance, to avoid rejection or just to please. You may avoid a current battle, but you have only postponed the war.

Many adult children are masters at manipulation and one of their schemes is to guilt trip you into assuming responsibility for them, their family, kids, bills, failures, happiness and security. As a general rule, do not do for them what they are fully capable of doing for themselves. Unnecessarily assuming their responsibilities is usually an effort to protect yourself and exert a subtle form of control. It can temporarily protect you, but it will only postpone the pain of the conflict. It will also enable them to continue to be irresponsible. Adults at any age are responsible for their own circles of responsibility. Yet God does not bless these first three steps. He has only promised to bless the next one.

Fulfill Your Circle of Responsibility

Here is the heart of power and change; it is the power of personal responsibility. The process of identifying, assigning and assuming responsibility does not work without the final step; fulfilling what is in your circle of responsibility. This is where you restore power and control to your life and possibly begin to heal fractured relationships

The first book written in the New Testament was the book of James. In the first chapter, God defines the basis to receive His blessing. "Prove yourselves doers of the Word, and not merely hearers who delude themselves, but one who looks intently at the perfect law... and abides by it, not having become a forgetful hearer but an effectual doer; this man shall be blessed in what he does" (James 1:22, 25). This explains why relationships fail. We confuse "knowing" with "doing" and deceive ourselves that we are doing. God does not bless the "knowers", "assigners" or "assumers". God only blessed the doers (Matt. 7:21).

Remember the Benefits of Being a Doer

Fulfilling what is in your circle of responsibility as a parent will give you something practical to do and give you the direction in which to go. You will know what the next right thing to do is. Being a doer will give you purpose in life. You will not spin your wheels asking God to give you a purpose in life. The things in your circle are your purpose for life and for His glory. By doing this, you will get a sense of accomplishment. Often, a parent will ask if they are getting anywhere. The answer is simply, "Are you doing what is in your circle of responsibility?" Those are the positive steps in the right direction. It will result in reducing tension and anxiety and give you a sense of security. It can rebuild relationships and leave you with a general sense of well being and peace.

They May Not Reconcile with You

The Apostle Paul's last words of counsel to Timothy were to prepare him for what it was going to look like near the end of time before our Lord Jesus returns. He said people will be self-centered, proud, ungrateful, unholy and unloving. Then comes the hardest one regarding relationships - people will be unforgiving or irreconcilable (2 Tim. 3:3).

The Greek word "*irreconcilable*" is a picture of two warring generals meeting to seal a treaty. One general pours a cup of wine upon a stone altar to symbolize that he accepts the terms of peace. But the other general decides he is not going to accept the terms of peace and he throws his drink offering on the ground. The word "irreconcilable" literally means "without libation" or without a drink offering of wine poured out upon an altar to seal the treaty.

You can do everything in your circle of responsibility and your grown kids could still choose not to be responsible or to walk away or just not change. But God knows and understands that people are sometimes just outright stubborn and refuse to be reconciled or cooperative. Paul explains this reality to the Corinthian church as it relates to marriage. If believers do all they can to live out their new faith and changed life, and their unbelieving spouse still wants to leave, God said let them go. Why? He has called us to peace (I Cor. 7:15). God has a special blessing for those who assume and fulfill their responsibility to be peacekeepers. He even gives them a special title, "sons of God" (Matt. 5:9). It is important to remember you will only be held accountable to God for what is in your circle of responsibility (I Cor. 5:10; Rom. 14:10).

It may seem unfair that only you are being the responsible one. But that is better than no one. Yes, it is unfair, but life in a sin-filled and fallen world is unfair. You can be at peace yourself, with or without your adult children's cooperation. Why? Because peace is a manifestation of the Holy Spirit in your life and is not dependent on the cooperation of your kids (Gal. 5:22). You may experience sadness because of the adult child's failure to grow up and be responsible, but sadness is an appropriate emotional response for his failure. Your task is to do what is in your circle of responsibility, then, having done all you can do, "to stand" firm (Eph. 6:13) and trust God for the results (Prov. 3:5,6).

Entrust Yourself to God

Before he died, the Apostle Peter gave his parting advice on how to deal with conflict when you have done all you can and there is no change and you have experienced some genuine hurts. He urged you to follow in the steps of Jesus who left you a pattern to follow. You do not have to ask, "What would Jesus do?" Peter told us what He did. When Jesus was verbally abused, He did not return the verbal abuse. When he was physically abused, He did not retaliate with threats. What did He do? "He committed Himself to Him (His Father) who judges righteously" (I Peter 2:23).

Did Jesus do this once and for all? No. The verb "committed" means He had to re-commit Himself to His Father repeatedly. What did He say? Father, You know what just happened here. It hurt! But I recommit myself to your understanding because I know you are a fair and righteous judge. Robert and Bev learned to do that when they received one negative response after another with each attempt they made to build a bridge with their daughter. Many times they just had to bow their heads in prayer and give themselves over to God and thank Him that they knew He understood.

Get Ready to Go

The journey to an improved relationship with your adult child may be a little bumpy at first, but you can trust God to give you the strength you need if you ask. It will take time so be patient with yourself and them. Change is not easy. Here are some questions to ask yourself to make sure you are heading in the right direction.

How have you adjusted your perspective regarding who you are and who your grown kids are? Are you finding yourself now talking to them adult-to-adult or do you still feel stuck in the parent/child rut? Have you been able to make a special effort to share your well-earned wisdom in such a way that they can listen and feel free to not accept it?

From a position of emotional maturity, have you taken the time to clarify your mutual expectations while maintaining a clear conscience before them? Has your adult child begun to feel genuinely loved by you from *his* perspective (if it is a healthy perspective)? Does the sphere of that love reflect your healthy boundaries?

Have you re-evaluated how you are dispensing your finances wisely while allowing the kids to experience need so they can learn to look to God to provide that need? Since grandkids are your joy and you want the absolute best for them, are you still free to let their parents be the parents? If you now have them to raise, can you picture God using you to give them a godly environment that could change their destiny?

Finally, do you have a better picture of what is in your circle of responsibility? Have you honestly looked at all aspects of your relationship with your kids? Have you assigned what is legitimately yours and assumed responsibility for it? Have you purposed in your heart, with God's help, to fulfill what is in your own circle of responsibility and keep entrusting yourself to Him?

Many months after our counseling time, I heard from Robert and Bev. They made a great effort to use these keys in their relationship with their daughter. She left home as a child. After much talking, confessing, crying and rebuilding, they mended the broken fences and healed the wounded hearts. She returned home as a temporary nester. It wasn't long before she was able to leave home as the healthy adult that Robert and Bev always dreamed she would be. My friend, it's not too late. You, too, can build a better relationship with your adult children.

CHAPTER 11

Points to Ponder

1. Identify what is or has been happening in the relationship.
2. Assign responsibility for the parts.
3. Assume responsibility for your parts.
4. Fulfill what is in your circle of responsibility
5. Remember God only gives grace for the truth.
6. Acknowledge areas in which you have failed and correct them.
7. Allow your kids to assume their own circles of responsibility.
8. Take an accurate x-ray of the family relationships.
9. Realize your best efforts may fail.
10. Avoid shifting your blame to others and taking blame for what you're not responsible for.
11. Remind yourself of the benefits of fulfilling what is in your own circle of responsibility.
12. Accept the reality that your kids may not want to be reconciled with you.
13. Entrust yourself to God daily.

CHAPTER 11

Resolve Conflicts Biblically

Small Group Questions

1. What obstacles have you overcome to acknowledge a hard reality regarding your adult children or yourself? If you were in denial, how did you get out of it?

2. How has assigning appropriate responsibility to either yourself or your grown kids made a positive difference for you?

3. What have you experienced with your adult children shifting blame to you for their behavior? How did you respond? How was your response received by them?

4. What "log" have you removed from your own eye in dealing with your kids? How did you come to realize there were things you were doing that were not helpful to your relationship?

5. What responsibilities of your adult children have you assumed in the past in order to gain peace, avoid guilt, gain their acceptance, avoid rejection or just please them? How did it work for you? What did you learn through this experience? What would you share with other parents who are now doing this?

6. Share the personal benefits you have experienced by fulfilling what was in your circle of responsibility related to your kids.

7. Describe your efforts to reconcile or build a better relationship with your adult children that did not produce the positive end you had hoped for. What have you done for yourself to accept this difficult situation?

8. Describe situations you went through with your grown kids that caused you to draw closer to the Lord. What scripture became very important to you?

9. What tools you are now using that have improved relationships with your adult children?

10. What opportunity have you had to share what you've learned with other frustrated parents? What was their response? What can you thank God for now?

Notes

Chapter 1

1 Ross Campbell and Gary Chapman, *Parenting Your Adult Child* (Chicago: Northfield Publishing, 1999), 12.

2 Selwyn Hughes, *Helping People through Their Problems* (Minneapolis: Bethany House Publishers, 1981), 6.

3 Edwin Klingelhoffer, *Coping with Your Grown Children* (New York: Humana Press, 1989), 154.

4 Larry Stockman and Cynthia Graves, *Grown-Up Children Who Won't Grow Up* (Rocklin, CA: Prima Publishing, 1990),1.

5 Edwin Klingelhoffer, *Coping with Your Grown Children, 17.*

6 Stockman and Graves, *Grown-Up Children Who Won't Grow Up, 37.*

7 Stockman and Graves, *Grown-Up Children Who Won't Grow Up*, 18.

8 Valerie, Wiener, *The Nesting Syndrome: Grown Children Living at Home* (Minneapolis: Fairview Press, 1997), 49.

9 Robert Hemfelt and Paul Warren, *Kids Who Carry Our Pain: Breaking the Cycle of Codependency for the Next Generation* (Nashville: Thomas Nelson Publishers, 1990), 28.

10 Campbell and Chapman, *Parenting Your Adult Child,* 140.

Chapter 2

11 Robert Hemfelt and Paul Warren, *Kids Who Carry Our Pain: Breaking the Cycle of Codependency for the Next Generation* (Nashville: Thomas Nelson Publishers, 1990), 253.

12 Eric Berne, *Transactional Analysis in Psychotherapy* (Secaucus: Grove Press, 1961).

13 Valerie Wiener, *The Nesting Syndrome: Grown Children Living at Home* (Minneapolis: Fairview Press, 1997), 121.

14 Ross Campbell and Gary Chapman, *Parenting Your Adult Child* (Chicago: Northfield Publishing, 1999), 141.

15 Valerie Wiener, *The Nesting Syndrome,* 121.

16 Campbell and Chapman, *Parenting Your Adult Child,* 31.

17 Shauna Smith, *Making Peace with Your Adult Children* (New York: Harper Perennial, 1991), 87.

[18] Valerie Wiener, *The Nesting Syndrome*, 118, 119.

[19] Campbell and Chapman, *Parenting Your Adult Child*, 155.

[20] Shauna Smith, *Making Peace with Your Adult Children*, 115.

[21] Shauna Smith, *Making Peace with Your Adult Children*, 183.

[22] Harriet Lerner, *The Dance of Anger: A Woman's Guide to Changing the Pattern of Intimate Relationships* (New York: Harper and Row Publishers, 1985), 20.

[23] Campbell and Chapman, *Parenting Your Adult Child*, 31.

[24] Campbell and Chapman, *Parenting Your Adult Child*, 31.

[25] Shauna Smith, *Making Peace with Your Adult Children*, 81.

[26] Valerie Wiener, *The Nesting Syndrome*, 160.

Chapter 3

[27] Edwin Blum, *The Bible Knowledge Commentary New Testament: An Exposition of the Scriptures*, ed. John F. Walvoord and Roy B. Zuck (Wheaton, IL: Victor Books, 1983), 328.

[28] Ross Campbell and Gary Chapman, *Parenting Your Adult Child* (Chicago: Northfield Publishing, 1999), 142.

29 Ross Campbell and Gary Chapman, *Parenting Your Adult Child* (Chicago: Northfield Publishing, 1999), 145.

Chapter 4

30 Larry Stockman and Cynthia Graves, *Grown-Up Children Who Won't Grow Up* (Rocklin, CA: Prima Publishing, 1990), 20.

31 Shauna Smith, *Making Peace with Your Adult Children* (New York: Harper Perennial, 1991), 299.

32 Shauna Smith, *Making Peace,* adapted, 323.

33 Shauna Smith, *Making Peace,* adapted, 324.

34 Shauna Smith, *Making Peace,* adapted, 325.

35 Shauna Smith, *Making Peace,* adapted, 298.

36 Edwin Klingelhoffer, *Coping with Your Grown Children* (New York, Humana Press, 1989), 110.

37 Edwin Klingelhoffer, *Coping,* 154.

38 Barbara Johnson, *Where Does a Mother Go to Resign?* (Minneapolis: Bethany House, 1979), 10.

[39] Anita Worthen and Bob Davies, *Someone I Love is Gay: How Family and Friends Can Respond* (Downers Grove: InterVarsity Press, 1996), 24-26 Adapted.

Chapter 5

[40] Shauna Smith, *Making Peace with Your Adult Children* (New York: Harper Perennial, 1991),172.

[41] Larry Stockman and Cynthia Graves, *Grown-Up Children Who Won't Grow Up* (Rocklin, CA: Prima Publishing, 1990), 88.

[42] Phil Waldrep, *Parenting Prodigals: Six Principles for Bringing Your Son or Daughter Back to God* (Friendswood, TX: Baxter Press, 2001).

[43] Stockman and Graves, *Grown-Up*, 159.

[44] Shauna Smith, *Making Peace*, 23-24, adapted.

[45] Shauna Smith, *Making Peace*, 237.

[46] Harriet Lerner, *The Dance of Anger. A Woman's Guide to Changing the Pattern of Intimate Relationships* (New York: Harper and Row Publishers, 1985), 133.

[47] Lerner, *Dance of Anger*, 203.

48 Shauna Smith, *Making Peace,* 5.

49 Stockman and Graves, *Grown-Up Children,* 13.

Chapter 6

50 John Friel and Linda Friel, *Adult Children: The Secrets of Dysfunctional Families* (Deerfield Beach, FL: Health Communications, Inc, 1988), 89, 90.

51 James Friesen, E. James Wilder, Anne Bierling, Rick Koepcke, Maribeth Poole, *The Life Model: Living from the Heart Jesus Gave You* (Kerney: Morris Publishing), 6.

52 Hemfelt, Robert, Paul Warren, *Kids Who Carry Our Pain: Breaking the Cycle of Codependency for the Next Generation* (Nashville: Thomas Nelson Publishers), 89.

53 Valerie Wiener, *The Nesting Syndrome: Grown Children Living at Home* (Minneapolis: Fairview Press, 1997), 101.

54 Friesen, Wilder, Poole, Koepcke, Bierling, *The Life Model,* 16.

55 Larry Stockman and Cynthia Graves, *Grown-Up Children Who Won't Grow Up* (Rocklin, CA: Prima Publishing, 1990), 60.

56 Harriet Lerner, *The Dance of Anger: A Woman's Guide to Changing the Pattern of Intimate Relationships* (New York: Harper and Row Publishers, 1985), 39.

57 Stockman and Graves, *Grown-Up Children,* 75.

58 Valerie Wiener, *The Nesting Syndrome,* 136.

59 Les Carter, *Good and Angry* (Grand Rapids, Michigan: Zondervan Publishing House, 1983), 28.

Chapter 7

60 Shauna Smith, *Making Peace with Your Adult Children* (New York: Harper Perennial, 1991), 183.

61 Ross Campbell and Gary Chapman, *Parenting Your Adult Child,* (Chicago: Northfield Publishing, 1999), 153.

62 Campbell and Chapman, *Parenting Your Adult Child,* 148.

Chapter 8

63 Robert Hemfelt, Paul Warren, *Kids Who Carry Our Pain: Breaking the Cycle of Codependency for the Next Generation* (Nashville: Thomas Nelson Publishers), 181.

64 Henry Cloud and John Townsend, *Boundaries* (Grand Rapids: Zondervan Publishing House,1992), 29.

65 Henry Cloud and John Townsend, *Boundaries,* 29.

66 Shauna Smith, *Making Peace with Your Adult Children (*New York: Harper Perennial,1991), 279.

67 John Friel and Linda Friel, *Adult Children: The Secrets of Dysfunctional Families* (Deerfield Beach, FL: Health Communications, Inc, 1988), 58.

68 John Friel and Linda Friel, *Adult Children,* 59.

69 Robert Hemfelt, Paul Warren, *Kids Who Carry Our Pain,* 15.

70 Robert Hemfelt, Paul Warren, *Kids Who Carry Our Pain,* 180.

71 Ross Campbell and Gary Chapman, *Parenting Your Adult Child,* (Chicago: Northfield Publishing, 1999), 58.

72 Valerie Wiener, *The Nesting Syndrome: Grown Children Living at Home* (Minneapolis: Fairview Press, 1997), 48.

73 Ross Campbell and Gary Chapman, *Parenting Your Adult Child,* 60-61.

74 Henry Cloud and John Townsend, *Boundaries,* 34.

75 Larry Stockman and Cynthia Graves, *Grown Up Children Who Won't Grow Up,* (Rocklin, CA: Prima Publishing, 1990),15.

76 Robert Hemfelt, Paul Warren, *Kids Who Carry Our Pain,* 253.

77 Valerie Wiener, *The Nesting Syndrome,* 21.

78 Ross Campbell and Gary Chapman, *Parenting Your Adult Child,* 57.

79 Ross Campbell and Gary Chapman, *Parenting Your Adult Child,* 47.

80 Ross Campbell and Gary Chapman, *Parenting Your Adult Child,* 94.

81 Ross Campbell and Gary Chapman, *Parenting Your Adult Child,* 96.

82 Anita Worthen and Bob Davies, *Someone I Love is Gay: How Family and Friends Can Respond* (Downers Grove: InterVarsity Press, 1996), 115.

83 Ross Campbell and Gary Chapman, *Parenting Your Adult Child,* 97.

84 Ross Campbell and Gary Chapman, *Parenting Your Adult Child,* 96.

85 Ross Campbell and Gary Chapman, *Parenting Your Adult Child,* 95.

86 Larry Stockman and Cynthia Graves, *Grown Up Children,* 7.

87 Ross Campbell and Gary Chapman, *Parenting Your Adult Child,* 99.

88 Ross Campbell and Gary Chapman, *Parenting Your Adult Child,* 105.

Chapter 9

89 Larry Stockman and Cynthia Graves, *Grown-Up Children Who Won't Grow Up* (Rocklin, CA: Prima Publishing, 1990), 42.

90 Henry Cloud and John Townsend, *Boundaries* (Grand Rapids: Zondervan Publishing House, 1992), 126.

91 Larry Stockman and Cynthia Graves, *Grown-Up Children,* 38.

92 Edwin Blum, *The Bible Knowledge Commentary New Testament: An Exposition of the Scriptures,* ed. John F. Walvoord and Roy B Zuck (Wheaten, IL: Victor Books, 1983), 723.

93 Valerie Wiener, *The Nesting Syndrome: Grown Children Living at Home* (Minneapolis: Fairview Press, 1997), 130.

94 Ross Campbell and Gary Chapman, *Parenting Your Adult Child,* (Chicago: Northfield Publishing, 1999), 125.

95 Ross Campbell and Gary Chapman, *Parenting Your Adult Child,* 126.

96 Larry Stockman and Cynthia Graves, *Grown-Up Children,* 32.

97 Edwin Klingelhoffer, *Coping with Your Grown Children* (New York: Humana Press, 1989), 143.

Chapter 10

98 Ross Campbell and Gary Chapman, *Parenting Your Adult Child,* (Chicago: Northfield Publishing, 1999), 115.

99 Edwin Blum, *The Bible Knowledge Commentary New Testament: An Exposition of the Scriptures,* ed. John F. Walvoord and Roy B Zuck (Wheaten, IL: Victor Books, 1983), 774.

100 Shauna Smith, *Making Peace with Your Adult Children (*New York: Harper Perennial, 1991), 73.

101 Ross Campbell and Gary Chapman, *Parenting Your Adult Child,* 314.

102 Shauna Smith, *Making Peace with Your Adult Children,* 114.

103 Shauna Smith, *Making Peace with Your Adult Children,* 317, 318.

104 Shauna Smith, *Making Peace with Your Adult Children,* 381.

105 Ross Campbell and Gary Chapman, *Parenting Your Adult Child,* 118.

106 Shauna Smith, *Making Peace with Your Adult Children,* 317.

107 Valerie Wiener, *The Nesting Syndrome: Grown Children Living at Home* (Minneapolis: Fairview Press, 1997), 62.

108 Ross Campbell and Gary Chapman, *Parenting Your Adult Child,* 121.

109 Valerie Wiener, *The Nesting Syndrome,* 64.

110 Edwin Klingelhoffer, *Coping with Your Grown Children* (New York: Humana Press, 1989), 99.

Chapter 11

111 John Friel and Linda Friel, *Adult Children: The Secrets of Dysfunctional Families* (Deerfield Beach, FL: Health Communications, Inc, 1988), 101.

112 Ross Campbell and Gary Chapman, *Parenting Your Adult Child,* (Chicago: Northfield Publishing, 1999), 141.

For additional learning opportunities please visit:

http//www.drchucklynch.com

Made in the USA
Charleston, SC
15 October 2011